"RADIATION"
THE SILENT KILLER

"RADIATION"
THE SILENT KILLER

NUCLEAR AND CHEMICAL RESEARCH INVOLVING OUR MILITARY PERSONNEL
in the development of the Atomic Bomb

Researched and Written

By

Albert G. "Smoky" Parrish

Founder of
"THE FORGOTTEN 216th"

ISBN 1-58500-389-1

1stBooks-re.04/20/00

About the Book

This book has personal experiences of men in the Military that had the Highest U.S Government Security Clearance. Our jobs were TOP SECRET and until the records were unaeled by Secretary Hazel O' Leary on December 6, 1993, we were sworn to secrecy , and forbidden to talk about our role in the Atomic Bomb testing, for reason of security or espionage. Our medical records were also sealed in the "Top Secret" category of Government records. Our outfit distributed and developed the film badges that were AVILABLE to us. We also decontaminated all humans and equipment, mapped the radiation, at ground zero and fallout, retrieved all scientific instruments, near ground zero immediately after the shot. We were called "RADIATION MONITORS," OUR SECURITY WAS CLASS "Q CLEARANCE," which was **the** Highest Security Clearance in the United States of America.

This research is dedicated to the Veterans who have died, also those having physical or emotional problems from their Military involvement with Radiation Testing, or their association with chemicals, while they were in the service of their country.

Also, I would like to acknowledge and thank the following:

My wife "Orie" for her faithful help, support and sacrifice;

The Honorable United States Senator Paul David Wellstone, along with his Legislative Fellow, Dr. Martin Gensler, and also Josh Syrjamaki, His Labor and Veterans Liaison for their never-ending support, help and encouragement.

The U.S. Army's 216th Chemical Service Company's Veterans, and "The Forgotten 216th." Without their help and information this research would not have been possible.

Albert G. (Smoky) Parrish

Albert G. (Smoky) Parrish
P.O. Box 236
Hackensack, MN 56452

A letter to my readers:

The reason for writing this book is to prove, by their own records, how slip-shod Our U.S. Government is acting. They are trying to reconstruct from other sources, the "ACCURATE" amount of Radiation that each Person in the Military received from their part serving our Country in the Atomic Bomb Tests.

The 1998 fiscal year budget for the NTPR alone, (Nuclear Test Personnel Review) is an amazing $7.23 Million. This has been ongoing for 20 years, just to keep 16,630 Atomic Veterans from receiving the health care and compensation they rightly deserve. In reality the $7.23 million would pay for these benefits.

To take a film badge reading, or Radiation dosage from one person, when the NTPR has no idea where that person was located during that test. Then give that dosage to another person as an "accurately" reconstructed dosage, for their health records, for the rest of their life. This is ABSOLUTELY RIDICULOUS. Would you give 1 guard out of every 6 guards at a Nuclear plant a film badge, on an average of 1 out of every 12 days they worked, and call this an "ACCURATE" measure to diagnose the illnesses of everyone that had worked in that plant? I think you would be senile to take a dosage from some individual, not knowing if they were sleeping in a vehicle, or where they were, and give that very same measurement to a person mapping Ground Zero. This is the theory used by the NTPR to shape our lives on.

We the 216th Chemical Service Company, were the ones that monitored, mapped and decontaminated all of the Radiation in the Tumbler-Snapper tests in 1952. Some of our tests were more than twice the power of the Atomic Bomb that devastated Hiroshima, Japan, and killed over 100,000 people.

Even though we were in the most Radiation contamination in these tests, 45% of us, in 91 days never received a single film badge and the 74 that were recorded with film badges, only got 7 to 11 film badges in the complete duration of the 91 days. No one knows how many of the 74 were "reconstructed" by the NTPR. Our government is getting by with this kind of fortune telling.

I personally DO NOT feel like I was used as a Guinea Pig. I feel I was a part of the Military personnel to gain superiority in the technology of Nuclear War used to win our freedom in World War II, and maintain that superiority to this date. Even though we served our Country During the Korean War, we were pioneers in the Nuclear Testing. Out of 1051 tests by the U.S. we took part in the 25th through the 32nd tests. The first 24 tests include the 2 Atomic Bomb Dropped on Japan to end W.W.II.

Albert G. (Smoky) Parrish

I would like to quote a paragraph from this book,
the book is distributed through the,
UNITED STATES GENERAL ACCOUNTING OFFICE
BOOK NUMBER 134247
Report to the Chairman, Committee on
Veterans Affairs, U. S. Senate

NUCLEAR HEALTH AND SAFETY
Radiation Exposures for
Some Cloud-Sampling
Personnel Need to Be
Re-examined..

I WILL QUOTE FROM PAGE THREE PARAGRAPH ONE.

Paragraph Title;
ACCURACY OF FILM BADGES AND FILM BADGE
EXPOSURE RECORDS.

Film badges are the official record of personnel
exposure to external radiation for those who participated
in the atmospheric Nuclear Weapons Testing Program.
However, <u>problems were identified with some of the
film badges used. particularly at</u> **OPERATION
TUMBLER-SNAPPER AND RED WING.** For
instance, about 10 years after the film badge's use at
Tumbler-Snapper, the manufacturer reported that the
badges two film components could not effectively
measure radiation between 4 & 9 rem.

GAO/RCED-87-134   (87 PAGES)

INDEX
"RADIATION" THE SILENT KILLER.

70. Richard Granger; Monitor and Decontaminated Vehicles.
71. Richard Hallen; Inexperienced Driver and was not trained in the affects of Radiation.
72. Gerald Fisher; Non-Commissioned Officer in Charge of Decontamination. Ground Zero Monitor.
72. Roman Mamer; Radiation Monitor.
74. Don Arntz; Radiation Monitor and developed film badges
75. Albert Parrish; Monitoring and tracking the Fallout.
77. Robert Arnet; Aircraft Radiation Monitor and Radio Operator. Also Setting up and operating Air Samplers.
78. Albert Parrish; Sent out to see how much radiation fallout two of us could collect on a film badge,
78. Norman Reiser; Maintained Radiation Filter station. Also was a Ground Zero and Fallout Monitor.
79. Charles Jameson; Ground Zero Radiation Monitor.
80. Walter Hyser; Monitor and Guard at Ground Zero
81. Leslie Full; Decontaminated Vehicles and personnel.
81. Warren Slavicek; Ground Zero Monitor and plotted all Radiation intensities on a map in Col. Day's office.
81. CLOSE friends whose families were compensated for their death from Radiation
82. Dick True; Decontaminated vehicles, and was also a Ground Zero Monitor.
83. Charles Huffman; Off-sight, Fallout Radiation Monitor.
83. Franklin Duester Ground Zero, Monitor and Guard. Also off site Fallout Air filter operator.
84. Richard Granger; Ground zero, offsite and personnel Radiation Monitor. Also vehicle decontamination.
84. Melvin Whitehead; Monitor of permanent Air Filter Stations.
84. Ronald Brower; Radiation Monitor at Ground Zero and and Vehicle decontamination.
85. Carl Lindgren; Radiation Overdosed at Ground Zero.

FILM BADGE RECONSTRUCTION-RIGHT(?) OR WRONG(?)

Some facts about your Radiation Dosage and how it was reached. This study was done with the only group of men that worked on FILM BADGES, if you were in the "Tumbler-Snapper Series in Nevada in 1952" because they were the ones that DISTRIBUTED, DEVELOPED, and RECORDED your film badge. That group, "AFSWP" (197 men), was also in charge of all DECONTAMINATION on VEHICLES, civilian and military PERSONNEL, and EQUIPMENT This group also did ALL of the MONITORING of Radiation, MAPPING around Ground Zero, the Fallout, and in the air within 340 KM. of the Nevada Proving Grounds.

AFSWP (Armed Forces Special weapons Project) 138 of 197 were 216th Chemical Service Company Personnel

If you knew the facts, I'm sure you would *NOT* be trying to get the U.S. Government to come up with your accurate dosage, because in my opinion, that would be impossible!!! In the first place, if the U.S. Government could RECONSTRUCT anyone's dosage, why not just issue one film badge for each shift at a Nuclear Plant?? After all, all of the personnel arc working in the same plant and location. Just think of the money the U.S. Government would save on Reconstructing our Film Badges ....

DON'T BE FOOLISH!!

Some of the reasons that Japan, with Hiroshima and Nagasaki, along with Chernobyl, Russia have so much better records, health care follow-up, and compensation on the people involved in the nuclear detonations is as follows.

Japan and Russia kept track and followed the health care and needs in their disasters. The United States didn't and some of the

1

individual United States Nuclear tests were 100 times more powerful than Hiroshima, Nagasaki, or Chernobyl.

The United States, on many occasions in almost every series of tests, hauled in thousands of military personnel and put them in trenches previously dug. These servicemen were not security cleared. The Army and Marines just hauled them in to the site in trucks from Desert Rock. This was a camp called "TENT CITY" or a staging area a couple of miles outside of Camp Mercury, the secured test site. After the detonation the trucks would arrive and load the men up, haul them out and return them to their former camps.

No one ever kept track of who they were, what physical or emotional problems they might have received from the radiation, or at what a young untimely life was given up without even recognizing that this person had Died serving their Country.

The facts are on page 123, It shows that the United States had a Total of 926 Nuclear tests at the Nevada test site. and a Total of 1,051 Nuclear tests by the U.S. worldwide. Think about it. Is Nevada, Bikini, or Aniwetoc any less contaminated than Japan or Russia, and yet the United States is paying to rehabilitate Japan and Russia including their medical bills from Nuclear disasters, oh what a disgrace to treat our own servicemen and women with this kind of contempt.

PAUL D. WELLSTONE
MINNESOTA

MINNESOTA TOLL FREE NUMBER
1-800-642-6041

COMMITTEES:
ENERGY AND NATURAL RESOURCES
LABOR AND HUMAN RESOURCES
SMALL BUSINESS
INDIAN AFFAIRS

United States Senate
WASHINGTON, DC 20510-2303

February 1, 1994

Mayor A. G. Parrish
P.O. Box 236
Hackensack, MN 56452

Dear Mayor Parrish:

I understand that you have met with or contacted my staff member, Scott Adams, regarding your experience as a member of the 216th Chemical Service Corps and your participation in Operation Tumbler Snapper in 1952 in Mercury Nevada. I was disturbed to be informed that members of the 216th Corps were ordered to monitor radiation fallout from atmospheric nuclear tests.

Today I met with Secretary of Veteran Affairs Jesse Brown and discussed the situation of the 216th Corps with him. Secretary Brown told me that he would assign one of his highest ranking staff members to come to Minnesota and meet with members of the 216th corps in the near future.

I feel that Secretary Brown's commitment to investigate the role of the 216th Corps will go a long way to answering some of the questions that you have raised with my staff. You certainly deserve answers from the Government as to why you were ordered to monitor radiation fallout without regard to your own health and safety.

I also hope the Government will use this important information to address the issue of compensation to those who have died

3

from being exposed to excessive radiation related medical conditions, yet they have had difficulty getting, or perhaps are still struggling to get V.A. coverage for their health problems.

I am inviting you and any other members of the 216th who may be interested to meet with me in my St. Paul office this Sunday, February 6 at 11:00 a.m. I want to hear about your experiences while serving your country at the Nevada Test Site. I will also be inviting the media to come to a press conference in my office at noon immediately following our meeting. If you want to share your experiences with the media, you are welcome to do so. Please refer to the attached page which has information about the meeting, including the address and directions to my office.

I believe that it is important to get the word out so we can begin to seriously address this issue. I also feel that media attention might reach other veterans who may have been exposed to radiation or reach the families of veterans who have died from disease caused by radiation exposure. If we are able to raise awareness and reach out to other veterans and the public, we will help work for justice for those who have served their country in an admirable way.

If you have any questions, please call Josh Syrjamaki of my staff at 645-0323. I look forward to meeting you this Sunday.

Sincerely,

Paul David Wellstone
United States Senator

PDW:sba

To those people who are unfamiliar with what radiation is and how you are exposed to it in the desert, I'll tell you what we understood it to be. First of all, you can not smell. See. or feel radiation. It is absorbed into personnel, equipment, dirt or anything else on earth. Most naturally the highest amount of contamination is absorbed into the dirt, only because there is more of it. At Sea the ship gets the largest contamination.

In order to Decontaminate personnel, equipment or vehicles we had only two things to decontaminate with, and that was soap and water. WE washed or showered the contamination (dust and dirt) off. However if the contamination has been on personnel or equipment for an extended period of time, or at a very high concentration, it is absorbed into the human body or material it has been on. Then after it has been washed and still has a high contamination, it will just have to sit until the radiation dissipates or evaporates. Sometimes you keep washing to try to hurry the process of decay. Some different types of radiation cells have a half life of thousands of years, and some has a half life of one hour..

To explain a little more about fallout it is a subject, we will have to learn a little about.

First of all we have to know how and where fallout originates, and fallout is just as dangerous as Ground Zero, After all Ground Zero is where the fall out originates. The tower shots, or the bombs sitting on a 300 foot steel tower carry the highest concentration of fallout, and it's contamination life is longer than an air drop bomb, because of the heavier material contaminated..

The heat from the explosion is so great that it literally MELTS the one inch thick steel legs of the tower, instantly. The heat again is so great, and if you look at the mushroom cloud, it is rising so fast in the center of the explosion that as the heat pushes upward, a part of the cloud is pushed outward taking on the appearance of a mushroom. The heat and center of the cloud, most all of the time, reaches a height of 35,000 to 50,000 feet above the ground, where it gets into the prevailing winds. (usually around 100 mph) these winds can be blowing in any direction, and depending on the weight of the material and speed of the winds determine the distance of travel before the radiation contaminated material falls out.

There is so much of an upward thrust that the closer large boulders on the ground are sucked towards Ground Zero.

If you read one of the three statements that I made in the 39 letters from our AFSWP group, in this book you will learn that the steel particles from the tower, dropped out over Groom Mine. The steel particles dropped into their overhead drinking water tank. (without a cover) and the whole mining area had to be evacuated, because of high concentration of radiation all around.

WE ATOMIC VETERANS ARE 70 YEARS OLD NOW! I ASK, HOW MUCH LONGER? A Congressional Investigation is needed for the Atomic Veterans on the accuracy of the film badge and the way it was used. The health care and compensation for an Atomic Veteran is based on the amount of radiation received during their work with the Atomic Bombs while they were in the service of their country.

My intention in this book is that I would like to prove that the film badge records for each Veteran were not the actual radiation dosages we received. However, the U.S. Government kept all of the proof of which happened on Nuclear testing with humans classified as "Top Secret" and sealed every record.

Three years ago, Secretary Hazel O'Leary opened the Top Secret Files on Human Experiments with Radiation. The Atomic Veterans have been trying to publicize what we have been trying to say for 40 plus years.

When we worked with the Atomic Bomb to gain the Nuclear Technology and to stay ahead of RUSSIA in the development of the Atomic Bomb, we had to "swear to secrecy," everything we learned or heard, and we had to throw away all of our notes and papers. The only thing we kept was our memory of what we did and learned.

QUESTIONS AND ANSWERS COVERED IN THIS BOOK!!

1. Was the Film Badge developed or read correctly?   NO!
2. Was the Film Badge recorded correctly?   NO!
3. Did some of the personnel have to stay behind when the tests were done to correct the Film Badge records?   YES!
4. Who made the decision, and how was the decision made concerning who received the Film Badges and who did not?
Book ADA 122-242, Page 136
5. Were Film Badges in 1952 issued to personnel on the same basis and laws of today?.   NO!
6. Were the majority of the personnel on site and taking part in the test NEVER ISSUED A FILM BADGE?   YES!
7. Were there any personnel that were on the same assignment, at the same time, that received different readings on their individual film badges?   YES!
8. Was anyone assigned to Work in a "HOT" (high radiation) area without a film badge?   YES!
9. Was the equipment the 216th used on assignment going to ground zero dependable?   NO!
10. Were the vehicles completely decontaminated when they came in "HOT" from the tests area?   NO!
11. On occasion when the Atomic Energy Commission ran out of "CLEAN" vehicles, were any vehicles put into service from the "HOT MOTOR POOL" that were still contaminated with high levels of radiation?   YES!
12. Not covered in this book: Why will a hospital not X-ray a pregnant woman if it doesn't cause birth defects? Why are claims limited to cancer?

My army career started December 3, 1950. I was transferred to the USAR (United States Army Reserves) on December 2, 1952. I received my discharge on December 14, 1956.

A group of men that left from Minneapolis on December 3, 1950 were from all around Minnesota. The majority of them were from the Minneapolis and St. Paul area. We numbered over one hundred. We were sent to Ft. Riley, Kansas, where we were merged with more army inductees, to make a total of 220 men. Those 220 men were shipped from Ft. Riley, Kansas to Rocky Mountain Arsenal at Derby, Colorado, which is now named Commerce City, Colorado. On about the 15th of December, 1950 we were attached to the "216th Chemical Service Company."

Since the 1950's through this time "RMA' has been known as the most polluted area in the Western Hemisphere. The U.S. Government started to clean this area up in 1955, and has been cleaning up the toxic waste ever since (43 years). It will not be cleaned up until approximately the year 2020 (Government projection), another 23 years, making a total of 66 years that RMA will be cleaning up this toxic dump. Also the army knew of crops being damaged because of ground water contamination and animals and fish dying because of the pollution 45 years ago, or February, 1952, when we were stationed there.

The U.S. ARMY knew of the off-site underground water contamination and in 1955 built a 93-acre pond, lined it with asphalt, and tried to stop the underground water contamination from spreading further on private property abutting Rocky Mountain Arsenal, and covered it up.

This and the Radiation from testing the Atomic Bomb are the two longest cover-ups in our United States in all of history since our country was settled.

We were stationed at Rocky Mountain Arsenal (RMA) for 2 years, with the exception of 3-1/2 months from the middle of March through the middle of June, 1952. During this time we were ordered to go to Mercury, Nevada. In Camp Mercury we took the major part in the radiation monitoring of eight Atomic

8

Bomb tests. Some of the bombs were more than twice the size of the bomb dropped on Hiroshima, Japan.

We monitored for radiation after the detonations at and around ground zero, and also the off-site air and ground monitoring of all cities within 340 km. of the test site. We located and monitored the fallout. We also distributed the film badges that were available, collected them, developed and recorded the amount of radiation on them. We decontaminated all personnel, vehicles, some protective clothing (coveralls), and equipment that came into "control point with water and "TIDE" soap. We issued and maintained vehicles from the "HOT' motor pool. We were in charge of all radiation safety. We were the "AFWSP" Unit.

THE SILENT KILLER

So far as I'm concerned, one of the reasons I have worked on this research was to demonstrate how arrogant the Government has been to the very people who served their country in time of war, by not giving the veterans who deserved Health Care and compensation what they deserved. We have to wonder how many veterans have suffered and died while the records of the Atomic Bomb (radiation testing) were sealed from July 16, 1945, for 49 years, until Secretary. Hazel O'Leary opened the sealed "TOP-SECRET" files to the public on December 7, 1993.

In the beginning, everything was "TOP SECRET," and all records of Physical testing and events were sealed by our Government. If anything needed to be covered up to protect a superior or friend from scrutiny, it would be, without the possibility of anyone ever seeing the records. In the records it says that everything was so top secret that even the "TOP SECRET" laws and rules were sealed, so that the operations managers didn't know what they could or couldn't do. Everything that was done by our supervisors was done on the same basis, and we heard it every time we turned around: "This is not to going to hurt you." "We don't have to tell anyone anything." "Why do they have to know, anyway?" In my own mind I will always believe that our superior officers were not informed and did not really, know the dangers to which they were subjecting the enlisted men and even themselves. They also believed that their superiors would not put them in harm's way intentionally. They were wrong!!

Sometimes in the field on some of the Atomic Tests, some of the scientists would argue with us (AFSWP), because they didn't want to leave the shot area when radiation levels were too high and they hadn't completed their experiments yet. Sometimes we had to threaten to drive away and leave them if they didn't get in the vehicle so we could go back to the Control Point.

America's struggle to be Number One in the Nuclear Race in the World is perhaps best reflected in a comment by Rear Admiral W.K. Meridenhall, a Senior Nuclear Weapons Officer who complained that the Bomb Test Scientists were wasting valuable time. In a memo recently released, Field Commander Meridenhall wrote on October 18, 1951... <u>"I'm not interested in the science of measuring Radiation. I merely want to know can the troops tolerate the Radiation to which they are being subjected for FIVE MINUTES OR FIVE DAYS?"</u>

I am not really provoked about what we had to do for our country. We were proud to have a part in our fight to maintain our freedom. Some men gave a lot more than those of us who survived-THEY GAVE THEIR LIVES. So we don't think we were mistreated during our time in the service. We also feel we did our part in staying ahead of Russia in Atomic Technology even if it cost our health or lives. What we are provoked at is that after we did our part, the Government turned its back on us and said "PROVE IT--THE RECORDS ARE SEALED," when it came to our hospitalization and compensation.

I guess the main point I'm trying to get across in all of my research is how poorly the FILM BADGE was used. I will try to explain by the Government's own books and records, how they did not use the film badges like the laws are today, and yet the Veterans Administration uses the film badge records they have to base our claims and dosage on.

ALL STATEMENTS ON THESE ARTICLES HAVE GOVERNMENT RECORDS PROOF.

Let's just compare today's standards on Film Badge usage against 1952 usage. Today, if you work in a Nuclear plant you receive a (ONE) film badge for every shift, or each day. This film badge has to be developed within 24 hours.

In 1952 the AEC said I had 11 Film Badges (reconstructed) in 91 days. So what amount of radiation did I receive in the other 80 days? By the way, we had our first ATOMIC TEST only 10 miles from the camp we lived in for 91 days. Every morning we swept the floor out, but water was hauled in by truck, so we weren't allowed to scrub the floors at all (according to proof by letter written April 25, 1952). We had no windows in the hut. We also had a laundry bag full of dirty contaminated clothes under our beds until laundry day. So did we need a film badge? Yes... Did we have one? No... We were not allowed to have a film badge in Camp Mercury. We had plywood over screen, so if you wanted air, you just propped the plywood up and the screen was viable. There was no roofing, just plywood roofs (photo available).

Let's go a step further. Today a badge is issued that cannot accidentally be turned with the wrong side of the badge facing out, to record the radiation-in 1952 the film badge was worn in the chest pocket, with the lead strip facing out. So what happened if you accidentally put it in your pocket wrong?? Or if you bent over and it fell out of your pocket?? You're right-NO reading or contamination on your record.

According to Government Records, quoting from page 136, "The On site Operations Officer determined daily requirements for film badges and pocket dosimeter for the groups taking part in the tests." "A DuPont type 558 film badge and one or more self-reading pocket dosimeters to official reentry parties and other personnel entering a controlled radiation area (an area with radiation intensities exceeding 0.01 Roentgens per hour)."

On Fox Shot from 25 through 31 May, according to records there were 10,600 personnel on the Tumbler-Snapper series and only 340 film badges were issued for the entire week of the shot. The majority of the Military Personnel, as you can see, didn't get a film badge. On this basis, how can the Government take the readings from these film badges, issued only on a hit or miss, or priority basis, and reconstruct a dosage amount for anyone else and call it accurate?

"Until 1955 film badges were issued to some of the personnel in a unit, such as a platoon, ship, or aircraft. If everyone in the unit was expected to receive similar exposures, only a few representatives might be badged. After 1955, DOD and AEC policy changed to require the badging of all participants. Some badges were environmentally damaged during their use and were rendered unreadable, and some records were lost or destroyed in the 1973 fire at the Federal Records Center in St. Louis.

"As a result, a significant portion of the NTPR (Nuclear Test Personnel Review) effort has focused on assessing the exposure of personnel who were not issued film badges and those whose records are missing or incomplete." (Page 46-1) (Underscoring Added.)

If you look at the facts and 50 years of hindsight, I think the tests were run in a sloppy manner, and would be ridiculed if today's business standards were used in judging them.

"Film Badges measure ONLY Gamma Radiation. The Radiation environment includes Neutron for close in personnel (indoor workers), Beta and Alpha Radiation (which cannot be measured on a film badge) for personnel whose activities indicate the possibility of inhalation or ingestion of radioactive materials (such as dust or dirt)." I ask myself--How do you measure the dust and dirt being ingested, if the film badge does

14

not record Alpha and Beta Radiation particles?? What I'm trying to say is, do you just take a given Radiation dosage and give a certain percentage to everyone? Or do you give more to the person that has to be brushed off with a broom at Ground Zero than you would give to an off-site monitor at a filter station? And finally, How can you tell in "dosage assessment" where each person was? Without each person having a film badge (pre-1955), I personally cannot understand how any dosage can be considered "true" or even accurate (throwing darts would be more accurate). In Book #122-242, Page 156, it says "the film badge was designed to measure the wearer's exposure to Gamma Radiation from external sources; the film badge was insensitive, however, to neutron radiation and did not measure the amount of Radioactive material that may have been inhaled or ingested." (Underscoring added)

The 216th Chemical Service Company (Army) had one of the most important jobs in this test. Out of 10,600 participants in the Tumbler-Snapper Series, only 197 personnel in this test were in the AFSWP group (Armed Forces Special Weapons Project) or in RAD-SAFE (Radiation Safety). Of the total 197 personnel 138 of them were from the 216th. AFSWP distributed, collected, developed, and recorded all film badges that were available to them. AFSWP was in control of all radiation monitoring and mapping from Ground Zero to 340 kin. of the test site, on the ground and in the Air, after each detonation, including fallout. AFSWP controlled all Radiation Decontamination of vehicles, equipment, and personnel civilian and military, that came from the test area, back through the Control Point.

AFSWP did cloud sampling on and off site, also the mapping of the radiation in the air. Filter stations in every major city were operated by the AFSWP monitors in the area of the stations. The monitors would meet Army planes at abandoned or private airports with filters they had changed from filter stations to be flown back to the control point, so the AEC could assess the amount of radiation in that particular area.

15

AFSWP (or the 216th) also had control of all decontamination of radiation on both the personnel and the vehicles. If the vehicles were HOT with radiation they were rinsed off on top and driving up on a rack, like a grease rack, with the front wheels approximately four feet higher than the rear wheels. A five-pound box of Tide soap was poured into a 55-gallon barrel of water, then the men pressure washed the underside of the vehicle with the soapy water. The contaminated dirt ran onto the ground and down a slight slope until it soaked into the ground.

There was no removal of the dirt under the washing area. If the radiation could not be satisfactorily removed from the vehicle, it was placed in what was called "THE HOT PARK" until some of the radiation dissipated and then it was washed again. It was then used again by the RAD-SAFE monitors. If vehicles were short, the vehicle was put back into service while it was still HOT.

The personnel washing the vehicles were constantly completely drenched from the washing of the vehicles. They DID NOT have any protective clothing or masks. We were told we didn't need that stuff. The wet contaminated clothing was worn back to Camp Mercury, dried in the hut, and then put into your laundry bag until wash day. The men on the "Decon" team didn't have film badges or dosimeters most of the time, because there weren't enough to go around. On page two it states, "A film badge and dosimeters were distributed to official reentry parties and other personnel entering a controlled radiation area (an area with radiation intensifies exceeding 0.01 Roentgens per hour)." Also from the same paragraph on page two, "The on-site operations office determined daily requirements for film badges for groups taking part in the tests."

The vehicles that could not be decontaminated by washing were put in the HOT PARK. The mechanic that worked on these vehicles to keep them in running order and also dispatched then had no film badge at all. It is hard to tell how much radiation he received.

Sometimes the dispatcher would have to send out HOT vehicles if he didn't have any vehicles that were decontaminated to a safe level the dispatcher did not have the authority to hold vehicles if someone had orders to use a vehicle out of the HOT PARK.

There are a few things I would like to mention about how we (Military Personnel) were used as Guinea Pigs. I really don't feel like I was used as a guinea pig. I feel it was a case of keeping AMERICA ahead of Russia's technology on the Nuclear Program. They were so close behind AMERICA in their development of atomic bombs, that we were glad to do our part, or even our lives to keep Russia from an attack on AMERICA. I would like to bring only two tests on humans to your attention. IN ALL OF THE RECORDS, I can only find four tests recorded on Military Personnel BUT you can be sure that if one guinea pig test was done on military personnel, there were many, many more done that we do not have information or knowledge about.

According to Book DNA 6020F, Pages 167-168, on project 4.5 flash blindness to determine how much the flash of a nuclear detonation impairs the night vision, 27 personnel were tested. Half had dark glasses and the other half had no glasses at all. I understand that after the fourth test, this project had to be discontinued because it damaged the retinas in their eyes.

There are letters from Veterans detailed in the next few pages. I, Albert Parrish, had orders and was sent out into the desert with another Army buddy to sit in the fallout of an atomic explosion to see how much radiation we could consume.

I got sick and laid down in the pickup but my buddy sat on the ground fifty feet away. His film badge recorded much more radiation than mine, I imagine because I was in the pickup. When we got back into the control point we were called into the office by the officers in charge because we had different readings on our film badges and were ordered to stay together.

This test as far as I am concerned was one of many guinea pig tests in this project. In the enclosed book you will find more information than I can describe in this letter. I would like you to

17

read the following material in this book, and then ask anybody from AFSWP personnel or anyone in the Forgotten 216th.

Sincerely and Respectfully,

Albert G. (Smoky) Parrish

Shields Warren, M.D., Director
Division of Biology and Medicine

November 28, 1950
(underscoring added by
U.S. Atomic Energy
Commission Albert G.
Parrish)

1901 Constitution Avenue, Washington 25, D.C.

Dear Shields:

Unfortunately, it will not be possible for me to be at the meeting on December 8, but I am passing along some of my ideas in the hope that they will be of some assistance to you and the others present at the conference.

To summarize briefly, in my estimation the biological equivalent "r" of 50 "r" Mev. total body-radiation* will probably provoke an appreciable, but not alarming degree of radiation sickness when given in a single dose. In other words, it would be my estimate, which is somewhat arbitrary as you must realize, that in the range of 25-50 "r" I would not anticipate a serious decrease in operational effectiveness of military or civilian personnel, assuming that they have been suitably indoctrinated and do not develop incapacitating symptoms on a psychological basis. The tendency for radiation sickness to appear would be significantly enhanced if the individual being exposed has been subjected to previous stresses such as prolonged physical effort, loss of sleep and other types of fatigue. Likewise one might expect some degree of enhancement of the radiation effect if the exposed individuals were subjected to the types of stresses indicated above. The biological equivalents of 150 "r" I expect would be pretty much of an incapacitating dose, but it would seem unlikely that there would be an appreciable number of fatalities, providing the individual did not have some concomitant injury from some other source. At the level of 350 "r", I would expect this to be M.L.D."50" figure. I should like to introduce an opinion that while my figures might be valid, there

19

will be many operational circumstances in which it will be difficult to predict the exposure that a group of individuals may have to undergo to perform a certain manipulation. However, it does seem to me appropriate that both the Atomic Energy Commission and the Armed Forces be given some numbers with a reasonable degree of reliability.

I suspect that one of the reasons you asked for me to be present was on the question of internal radioactive poisoning which is a field that I have a little more familiarity with than the problem of external irradiation. To summarize briefly, there are three principal routes by which radioactive substances, irrespective of their nature, may gain entry into the body. They are in decreasing significance; inhalation, oral ingestion and entry through abrasions, cuts, etc.

Of these three, inhalation is by far the most important. To indicate the number of millicuries inhaled that might be a crippling or lethal dose, of course, depends upon the radioactive agent, it's physical and chemical form, it's half-life, nuclear *(to Shields Warren M.D. Director A.E.C. page two)* characteristics, etc. There is much that we do not know about this problem, but as a representative figure I would expect that of the order of 10 millicuries of a radioactive element such as strontium '89', **if inhaled as a soluble aerosol and absorbed, would probably be close to the lethal range. This is based on the experience of Dr. Friedell** who many years ago gave a patient with widespread metasases from carcinoma of the breast 10 millicuries of a strontium '89' parenternal injection. **The patient nearly died** and best estimates that one can make would suggest that the bone marrow got of the order of several hundred roentgen. retention **Should the material inhaled be retained in the lung, it works out that The of 10 millicuries of a radio-element possessing the nuclear properties of strontium '89' would probably produce a severe and possibly fatal radiation injury to the pulmonary tissue.** To the best of our knowledge, the high degree of selective uptake noted in bone for so many radioelements is not observed in lymphoid tissue, notably spleen, unless the substance is administered in colloidal form. Likewise the gonads do not, to the best of my knowledge, show any unusual behavior towards fission products or materials that might be made radioactive on a large scale such as tantalum. Ablation of the thyroid requires about 50 millicuries of I'131' and this is not a likely hazard without much larger activities from other fission products being present.

As you will probably gather from the above comments, I have been speaking of immediate effects in the sense of disabling changes that might take place in the range from a few hours to a couple of months. **Long-term effects such as genetic changes, neutron induced cataracts, and carcinogenesis are a little more difficult to assess, and quite frankly under the present state of affairs, I feel that more concern should be given to the acute rather than to the chronic effect.**

It seems to me that it is very desirable to determine in man the range of total body radiation required to induce an appreciable decrease in his capacity to execute intricate tasks for which physical well being is essential. If this is to be done, it should in my estimation be not only total body radiation, but from Gamma rays in the I to 2 Mev energy level. For both political and scientific reasons, I think it would be advantageous to secure what data can be obtained by using large monkeys such as Chimpanzees which are somewhat more responsive than the lower mammals. Scientifically, the use of such animals bears the disadvantage of the fact that they are considerably smaller than most adult humans and a critical evaluation of their subjective symptoms is infinitely more difficult. If this is to be done in humans, I feel that those concerned in the Atomic Energy Commission would be subject to considerable criticism, as admittedly this would have a little of the <u>Buchenwald touch</u>. The volunteers should be on a freer basis than inmates in a prison. At this point I haven't any very constructive ideas as to where one would turn for such volunteers should this plan *To shields Warren M.D. Director A.E.C. page three* be put into execution. <u>There is much to recommend the use of adult males past the age</u>

21

of 50 in good physical status, however, one can't be certain that these people would respond in a similar manner to the 10 to 40 age group. **IN CONCLUDING, THE PICTURE AS I SEE IT IS TO ASCERTAIN WHAT IS THE DISABLING RANGE AND FACTORS WHICH MIGHT INFLUENCE IT.**

I trust that these comments may have been of some assistance to you, and again, I want to express my regret at not being able to be on hand for the meeting.

With very best regards,

Sincerely yours,

Joseph Hamilton, M.D.*

* In 1946, Dr. Hamilton was a member of the Committee for Review of Radiological Safety Measures. He was also a faculty member of the University of California at Berkeley.

By the time you have read this far, I am sure it is apparent that this book is based on proven facts and Government records. The preceding letter was at one time classified by the U.S. Government as "CONFIDENTIAL." This document has been released, and is now public information.

I hope this letter will be a reminder all the way through this book to sort out the real facts. These two doctors were a part of the Top Brass that were making decisions about Human Radiation Experiments.

We especially have to be concerned about paragraph two where it states, stresses and incapacitating symptoms on a psychological basis are possible." (Emphasis added) Later on it is told in Book ADA 122-242, Page 128-9 how the total indoctrination was to quote the Government records, "Finally, the Camp Desert Rock training aides were inadequate." Why then does the V.A. claim the only health effect from radiation is

CANCER? Why then can other service personnel have stress and psychological problems, but not the Atomic Veteran??

A little further into the letter, the doctor states that "internal radioactive poisoning, which is a field that I have a little more familiarity with than the problem of external radiation, consists of inhalation, ingestion, and through cuts and abrasions." "Of these three, inhalation is by far the most important. To indicate the number of millicuries inhaled that might be a crippling or lethal dose." Here again is another part of the V.A.'s claim that it is OK for other Veterans, but not Atomic Veterans. Again the U.S. Government claims only CANCER, NOTHING ELSE, IS CAUSED BY RADIATION.

Please consider that some of our buddies are paralyzed, one from a tumor inside of the spine. When you read the long-term effects such as lung problems, genetic changes, cataracts, and many, many more, there are more physical problems besides CANCER listed here.

This is the most important part of this letter; please remember that this doctor is one of the deciding factors in the experiments on our Military Personnel.

"If this is to be done in humans, I feel that those concerned in the Atomic Energy Commission would be subject to considerable criticism, as admittedly this would have a little of the "Buchenwald touch." (IN OTHER WORDS, BE CAREFUL TO COVER IT UP.) "The volunteers should be on a freer basis than inmates of a prison." "There is much to recommend the use of adult males past the ago of 50 in good physical status." In other words, the experiments are DANGEROUS.

For those of you who are not aware of what "Buchenwald" was, it was a German concentration camp that was active just several years prior to this letter where Jewish Prisoners experienced torturing experiments, such as injections of genus into the heart and body, also starvation, and any other experiment or torture that the Germans could think of. Most of the 6,000,000 Jews that were killed were tortured before they were burned alive in large furnaces, so the name

23

"BUCHENWAI.D" being used in association with our Atomic (experiments) or Tests, does not set well with anyone that was in the Military.

This letter as you can sec, is written to Shields Warren, M.D., and you will note that HE WAS THE DIRECTOR, or as I said "the Top Brass" in charge of the Atomic Energy Commission. Joseph Hamilton, M.D. was a member of the Committee for Review of Radiological Safety Measures. In other words, the author of the letter, J.Hamilton, M.D., was in charge of "the Rad-Safe Group" or "AFSWP" and what happened to the Personnel in the tests..

If Joseph Hamilton was in charge of the committee for Review of Radiological Safety Measures, why didn't he make sure we had film badges, protective clothing, dependable and safe equipment, and most of all he should have trained us on the dangers of radiation and its consequences ......

OR DIDN'T HE REALLY CARE?

PANEL FINDS WIDE DEBATE IN 40'S ON ETHICS OF RADIATION TESTS

By permission on Aug. 23, 1997 of
Phillip J. Hilts October 12, 1994 article

In the early years of the Cold War, a systematic effort to gain knowledge of the affects of radiation from experiments on human subjects was secretly planned at the highest levels of the United States Government. The number of experiments was some 10 times larger than known until now, but there was also more discussion than expected on the ethics of experimentation.

That is the outline of the complex picture being developed by the President's Committee on Human Radiation Experiments after 6 months of sifting through the archives of a dozen Federal agencies. The committee has brought to light a wealth of documents about the Governments behavior - sometimes furtive, sometimes ethical - that will force historians to rewrite part of the history of the dawn of the atomic age.

In particular, the advisory committee has traced the almost continual jostling between the military's desire for data on radiation and the ethical scruples of some senior officials. Since no clear operating policy emerged, the result was that some ethically dubious experiments were discouraged or disapproved, while others went ahead.

Last year, after the Albuquerque Tribune reported on a group of patients given high doses of radiation treatment for largely experimental purposes, Energy Secretary Hazel R. O'Leary responded by promising to open her agency's files, and President Clinton later ordered the committee to make a detailed inquiry into the experiments.

The Tribune article and the previous instances of unethical radiation experiments discussed by Representative Edward J. Markey, Democrat of Massachusetts, at Congressional hearings in 1986 suggested that a thorough search would extend the litany of horrific stories. They also raised questions as to what ethical guidelines, if any, had governed the experiments, and at what level in the Government the research program has been directed.

Dr. Ruth Faden, an ethecist at John Hopkins University who is the chairwoman of the committee, said: "Did we find new horror stories? Well, we know now that much more experimental work was done than anyone guessed."

While the radiation doses received by subjects in most cases were not large, at the time the hazards of low level radiation were not known, and consent was not usually sought.

But Dr. Faden did express surprise at the apparent deliberateness of the decision making. "Frankly, we did not believe before we started this that there was much debate and planning done in connection with these experiments." She said. "But there was, and it was at a high level of the-military and scientific establishment."

That is not to say what the motive was for these ethical discussions - whether it was high - minded moral reasons, or legal reasons or public relations reasons - but in any case there was an awareness at high levels that one could not proceed in the area of radiation and human experiments just casually. They took it seriously."

: Serious Talk About Need For Data :

Dr. Faden said that from the high level of Secretary of Defense on down through the secretaries of the Army, Navy and Air Force, there was serious discussion of the military's need for information about how dangerous radiation was to troops, how soldiers might react to it and what precautions were needed. The question was how to get that information, and how often were human experiments necessary.

"We are now piecing together the story of the past, an unexpected past, to help inform the future on these questions," she said. Among the papers unearthed by the committee are documents that show experiments were debated, planned and carried out in a layer of atomic medical bureaucracy by half a

26

dozen secret committees, which staff members estimate will increase the number of known experiments at least tenfold, to about 600. Most experiments involved exposing troops to varying amounts of radiation, usually without informing them of the risks or seeking their consent.

At the time, the documents suggest, being the subject of experiments was counted as one of the expected hazards of military life and training - not unlike subjecting soldiers to live fire in training exercises - and was not considered to be human experimentation.

The committee also found that, contrary to the belief that there was little debate about the ethics of such experimentation in the 1950's, Army ethical guidelines written in 1953 were in fact far stricter than the current rules.

But the rules - a nearly verbatim copy of the Nuremberg Code, a set of ethical principles that came out of the Nuremberg Trials after World War II - did not become operating guidelines, apparently because they were declared top secret.

One of the most important bits history found in the hundreds of thousands of documents so far received by the committee, Dr. Faden said, is that a fixture of current ethical debates whether it is possible to offer a patient honest treatment and experiment on him at the same time - appears to have been a consideration in even the earliest documents of Cold War experiments.

An Atomic Energy Commission memorandum dated April 17, 1947, recommends that human experimentation not be made public. "It is desired that no document be released which refers to experiments with humans and might have an adverse effect on public opinion or result in legal suits," it says. "Documents covering such work in this field should be classified 'secret'." The memorandum was also classified secret.

: Seeking Tests On Human Beings :

In the fall of 1947 the A.E.C., which later became the Nuclear Regulatory Commission, established a division of biology and medicine and the Advisory Committee on Biology and Medicine, made up of outside experts, to consider future human and animal experimentation.

Two years earlier, 18 patients - the subjects of the Albuquerque Tribune article - were injected with plutonium to help track its course in the body. The committee has found that in 1947 the military proposed that more systematic studies be conducted. While this was disapproved, some individual experiments, including the injection of radioactive material into humans, continued in June and July 1947.

After repeated requests from the military and private researchers to conduct radiation experiments on humans, Dr. Shields Warren, the chief medical officer of the A.E.C., said in July 1949 that he was "taking an increasingly dim view of human experimentation."

The debate continued on one track, but so did the experiments on another, in the absence of firm policy to the contrary.

In 1949 a group called The Joint Panel on the Medical Aspects of Atomic Warfare was created to oversee the atomic - related research in the Defense Department. In the minutes of a meeting of the panel, it was noted that if ethical rules were adopted, "then obviously a great deal of our present human tracer studies must be discontinued." Tracer studies involve injecting minute amounts of radioactive chemical to track the biochemical pathways of the chemical's metabolism in the body.

The minutes also noted that there were "ethical and medico-legal objections to the administration of radioactive materials without the patients knowledge and consent." And it said there would a greater culpability of the Government "if a Federal agency condones human guinea pig experimentation."

The defense Department tried to initiate experiments using atomic isotopes to conduct total body irradiation experiments on healthy human subjects. Officials of the A.E.C., Chiefly Dr. Warren, protested but soon relented.

Since the A.E.C. controlled the supply of radioactive materials, Dr. Warren was apparently able to block some of the worst experiments, which called for total body irradiation of healthy subjects.

But some researchers were able to get around the commissions objections. Hundreds of people were irradiated primarily at Universities, by using cancer patients who presumably might have benefited, or at least whose lives could not be greatly shortened by the experiments.

By 1951 it was clear to the military and their medical establishment that it would be necessary to answer in detail many questions about the affects of radiation on humans, and that soldiers would have to be used as guinea pigs.

In September of 1951 the joint panel on the Medical Aspects of Atomic Warfare prepared a memorandum saying that there were numerous reasons to conduct human experiments in atomic bomb explosions. And later documents show that at least four of the human experiments were carried out.

Using 'Volunteers' In The Military

Among the problems that required experiments on humans, the panel said, were whether atomic explosion caused changes in visual acuity or light blindness, whether radiation from explosions could-be measured in body fluids of people near such blasts whether any psychological damage might come from being near an atomic explosion and whether flight crews would have any important exposure if they flew near a nuclear blast. Each of these experiments were carried out.

(Next sentence added by A.G.Parrish)

(Ordered in Sept. 1951 all of these experiments were done in less than six months in the Tumbler-Snapper Series, Apr. 1952.)

One of the experiments, called Upshot-Knothole, included, "Subjecting 12 human volunteers and 700 rabbits to the initial light flash from 6 atomic detonations to investigate its effect on the visual function of the human eye and to determine the burn

29

injury processes in the dark-adapted rabbit eye." Military records show.

The military's use of the word 'volunteer' did not imply that informed consent was obtained.

In essence, the subjects were ordered to participate; they were not always told what the risks would be.

In other experiments, airplanes flew through radioactive clouds. A report on one such test, called operation Plumb Bob, begins, "The objective of this project was to measure the radiation dose, both from neutrons and Gamma rays, received by an air crew delivering an MB-1 rocket." Crewmen swallowed radiation film to help measure their exposure.

Another test was designed to see how well soldiers could perform after exposure to the flash of atomic detonation at night. "Human volunteers were dark-adapted in a light-tight trailer approximately 10 miles from the detonation. Their eyes were exposed to the flash. Some eyes were protected by a red filter, and some were unprotected."

The notes on the experiment said, "The project was terminated after shot 4 in order to evaluate the significance of lesions of the retina which were produced in two of the subjects."

About 42 officers were included in a "selected volunteer program" in which they watched the atomic blast from 2,000 yards away. (1 1/8 miles) In other experiments, troops were brought to within 5,000 or 7,000 yards of ground zero to watch atomic explosions, and were marched to the site of the explosion just after the bomb had gone off. It is not yet known what happened to the subjects of these and other experiments.

In February 1953, after 8 years of experiments without a consistent set of rules to govern them, Charles E. Wilson, then Secretary of Defense, prepared a memorandum saying that volunteers should be used as the-- only "feasible means for realistic evaluation and-or development of effective preventive measures of defense against atomic, biological or chemical

30

agents." The memorandum added, "The voluntary consent of the human subject is absolutely essential."

It recommended using the Nuremberg code which, if actually applied, would be stricter than current practices because it required detailed explanations of the hazards of experiments regardless of any claimed benefits, and allowed the subject to terminate experiments at any moment. But these guidelines remained so highly classified that few if any people below the secretaries of Army, Navy or Air Force were aware of them.

Staff members of the advisory committee said this created the zen-like question, "what is the effect of adopting ethical guidelines which are then kept Top Secret?"

Dear 216th Veteran,   April 10, 1996

**<u>I am writing this very important letter to get your help
to aid some of the 216th veterans with their V.A. claims...</u>**

I have a hearing with the Veterans Administration and I am
going to prove that in the early stages of Atomic Testing, we
were not adequately trained in: (1) the dangers of radiation; (2)
the necessity of the Film Badge; (3) the poorly kept dosage
records; and (4) in the case of 64 men out of 138 in our company
that were not issued one Film Badge during our tour of duty in
the tests.

Only three (3) years later, in 1955, the A.E.C. made new
guidelines and every, body. that was in the experiments or tests
was issued a Film Badge. The Government says in the records
that after 1955 <u>everyone was issued a film badge;</u> however, it
does not say whether the person was issued one film badge
during the whole test or whether the person was issued one film
badge every 24 hours, like they are issued in the Nuclear Plants
of today. To get the correct radiation reading the film badge
<u>MUST</u> be calibrated at the end of each shift of work.

I would like to quote a part of a letter I received from Roy B.
I would like to get a letter written similar to this of YOUR
opinion. I would appreciate it if you sent along an extra page of
remarks, but it is not necessary.

I am sending you two pages of questions, and the two pages
are all you have to return to me in my self-addressed envelope:

"Smoky, I worked on the film badges some, maybe I
can help a bit. I know the Monitor Readers got a film
badge, and Drivers also, to go out and read the radiation
lines fight after the blast. Then we got them to recover
dropped projects. If I remember, we just issued at the
Control Point Office. I think Name, Rank, and serial no.
so they could easily be identified. When they were
turned back in we read and recorded them. We put the
badges under a deal and it told us what the radiation

32

reading was. I worked in that office twice while in Nevada, then Commander Bussey either took or mailed them to Washington."

"Sam Johnson, Cleon Carpenter, Reed Kendal, myself and a young, fellow with the 216th, I can not recall his name stayed behind and **redone the records because they were all screwed up**." ROY BRACHT

The last paragraph is in reference to after all of the 216th left Nevada and went back to our home station in Denver, Colo.

All I am asking for is your own opinion and a response to this letter. At the hearing I am allowed to bring other witnesses and an attorney, if I want to.

I am sure that you are aware that we formed an organization (The Forgotten 216th), to help get hospitalization, medication, and compensation. We have accomplished this for some of the veterans and widows of former 216th Veterans. We have a long way to go yet to get some help for our Buddies. As you know, we have a hard time because a lot of the benefits arc based on the amount of radiation you had on your film badge, which is now a part of your "Radiation Dosage Records." In our Company alone (The 216th Chemical Service Company), 45 per cent, or 64 out of 138 men did not receive even one film badge in the 91 days we were stationed at Mercury, Nevada, working with the 1952 Atomic Bomb Tumbler-Snapper series tests (this information is documented by the U.S. Government).

Some of our buddies need wheel chairs, medical equipment, medical attention, and medicine. <u>In order to help them we have to tell the V.A. the facts as we know them</u>. So far as I am concerned, we did the best we could with the equipment that was available and the knowledge we had at that time.

Looking back 45 years, the Atomic Veterans are the only Veterans whose compensation is restricted either to the Film Badge or distorted facts that have never been corrected.

Just two days ago I was given a hearing with the V.A. The hearing will be in less than two months and I am in the process of trying to get a one-month postponement so that I can get the information that is sent to me recorded and organized for presentation to them (the V.A.).

I am only <u>asking you if you could give me the honest facts that you can remember.</u> I am sure that if we get the actual facts that the V.A. will take into consideration we were pioneers in Nuclear testing. There were only 23 Nuclear tests or experiments before ours. There were 1,029 tests after ours. I would consider our film badges and film processing to be (quoting from Government records)..."RELATIVELY CRUDE IN THE BEGINNING."

I need some information that you can provide me with, and I really need it fight away (May lst). U.S. Senator Paul Wellstone has worked for us in Washington, D.C. for benefits and recognition for the Atomic Veterans and has agreed to help us to the end.

P.S. I am enclosing a self-addressed envelope, but I do not know how many of these letters will find their destination and if any of them will be mailed back to me, so I am not going to put a stamp on the return envelope. If the forgotten 216th were sending these letters, they would probably stamp them, but I am having all of the answers returned directly to me, and we are 200 miles apart.

Sincerely and Respectfully,

Albert G. Parrish

QUESTIONNAIRE #1

NAME   TELEPHONE NO.   ZIP

ADDRESS   CITY   STATE

1. Did you work at the atomic test site in Nevada? Yes 45_ No 0
Didn't Know 0 .

2. How much training did you get to work on film badges or
radiation calibration?   Yes _____   Mos_____

3. Do you think you were as qualified during the tests as Didn't
Know people are doing the same job today with film badges?
Yes 0____   No__42____   __3__

4. How many days did you work on film badges in Nevada?
ANSWER ON SEPARATE PAGE

5. How many days did you work on film badge records in
Nevada?   ANSWER ON SEPARATE PAGE

6. Did you have any training with radiation before going to
Nevada? Yes__5____   No__39____   Didn't Know   __1__

7. Did you work on film badges or records during the tests?
Yes__9____   No__36____ Didn't Know   __-__

8. Did you work on film badges or records after the testing was
completed? Yes__7___ No__36____   Didn't Know__2__

9. Did the records have to be corrected after the testing was
completed?
Yes__10____   No__6____   Didn't Know   __30__

10. Do you think <u>ALL</u> radiation was read and recorded accurately?
Yes __0__   No __35__   Didn't Know   __11__

11. Was everyone at the site given a film badge?
Yes __4__   No __24__   Didn't Know   __17__
<u>ANSWER ON SEPARATE PAGE</u>

Please read this page out of one of the Gov't publications. It comes out of U.S. Department of Commerce, National Technical Information Book #ADA 122-242, Page 156. Again, there were only 23 tests ahead of Tumbler-Snapper Series and 1,029 tests on experimental atomic detonations after our tests.

If you know of someone that worked on film pages, please let me know their names.
<u>Also, if you can write one paragraph or more information about what you can remember, please add as much as you can and mail it back to me. Thanks, Smoky.</u>

Questionnaire #1 - Question #4.

All original letters are on file with Albert G. Parrish.

How many days in Nevada did you work on film badges?

1.	Gerald Bacon	NO ANSWER
2.	Ernest Kommer	NONE
3.	Raymond Hosfelt	NONE
4.	Hilmar Mayerhoffer	NONE
5.	Dick True	NONE
6.	Alan Daffer	NONE
7.	Robert Johnston	NONE
8.	Bob Opseth	NONE
9.	Stephen Demel	NONE
10.	Richard Miller	45 DAYS
11.	Ernest Trubl	NONE
12.	Joseph Slonka	NONE
13.	Wally Hyser	NO ANSWER
14.	Thomas Wethington	CAN'T REMEMBER
15.	Larry Hibben	NONE
16.	Eugene Toronto	NONE
17.	Stanley Johnson	30 DAYS AT LEAST-- 24-HOUR SHIFTS
18.	Paul Martin	TWO WEEKS
19.	Don Arntz	TWO OR THREE
20.	Minneapolis (unsigned)	FOUR
21.	Gerald Fisher	NONE
22.	Roy Bracht	FOURTEEN DAYS
23.	Norman Reiser	NONE
24.	Herbert Hong	NONE
25.	Richard Hallen	NONE
26.	R. Duane Kraft	NONE
27.	Franklin Duester	NONE
29.	Floyd Brittenham	THREE OR FOUR
30.	Richard Granger	NONE

37

31.	Melvin Whitehed	NONE
32.	Ardeen Zierott	NONE
33.	Unsigned	NONE
34.	Carl Lindgren	NONE
35.	James Fosnaugh	NONE
36.	Paul Miller	DON'T KNOW OR REMEMBER
37.	Gus Garcia	NONE
38.	Roman Mamer	NONE
39.	Paul L. Martin	DON'T RECALL
40.	Leslie Full	NONE
41.	Orville Huffman	NONE
42.	Albert Parrish	NONE
43.	John Slomba	NONE
44.	Larry Heintzman	NONE
45.	Elmer Floback	THIRTY DAYS

Questionnaire #1 - Question #5.

All original letters are on file with Albert G. Parrish.

How many days in Nevada did you work on film badge records?

1.	Gerald Bacon	NO ANSWER
2.	Ernest Kommer	NONE
3.	Raymond Hosfelt	NONE
4.	Hilmar Mayerhoffer	NONE
5.	Dick True	NONE
6.	Alan Daffer	NONE
7.	Robert Johnston	NONE
8.	Bob Opseth	NONE
9.	Stephen Demel	NONE
10.	Richard Miller	NINETY DAYS
11.	Ernest Trubl	NONE
12.	Joseph Slonka	NONE
13.	Wally Hyser	NO ANSWER
14.	Thomas Wethington	NONE
15.	Larry Hibben	NONE
16.	Eugene Toronto	NONE
17.	Stanley Johnson	NONE
18.	Paul Martin	TWO WEEKS
19.	Don Arntz	TWO OR THREE
20.	Minneapolis (unsigned)	NONE
21.	Gerald Fisher	NONE
22.	Roy Bracht	AT LEAST TWENTY-ONE DAYS
23.	Norman Reiser	NONE
24.	Herbert Hong	NONE
25.	Richard Hallen	NONE
26.	R. Duane Kraft	NONE
27.	Franklin Duester	NONE

29.	Floyd Brittenham	I HELPED SOMEONE TWO OR THREE DAYS
30.	Richard Granger	NONE
31.	Melvin Whitehead	NONE
32.	Ardeen Zierott	NONE
33.	Unsigned	NONE
34.	Carl Lindgren	NONE
35.	James Fosnaugh	LESS THAN A WEEK
36.	Paul Miller	NONE
37.	Gus Garcia	NONE
38.	Roman Mamer	NONE
39.	Paul L. Martin	DON'T RECALL
40.	Leslie Full	NONE
41.	Orville Huffman	NONE
42.	Albert Parrish	NONE
43.	John Slomba	NONE
44.	Larry Heintzman	NONE
45.	Elmer Floback	THIRTY DAYS

Questionnaire #1 - Question 11

All original letters are on file with Albert G. Parrish

Was everyone on the site given a film badge? (WRITTEN REMARKS)

4. Hilmar Mayerhoffer: There were days we didn't have any.
6. Alan Daffer: I worked with the monitors. Many times the badges were not consistent.
11. Ernest Trubl: I guess they figured they needed the film badges for going out in the "HOT AREAS."
12. Joseph Slonka: Some men got film badges, not all because there weren't enough to go around.
16. Eugene Toronto: Short supply.
17. Stanley Johnson: Everyone did not get a film badge. I think it was just sloppy government policy.
18. Paul Martin: Only those who went out in the field got the film badges.
21. Gerald Fisher: Film Badges were limited to certain jobs.
22. Roy Bracht: They (film badges) were all mixed up, wrong badges in wrong bags or storage bags. I heard lots never were issued film badges.
23. Norman Reiser: Not all had film badges. They didn't have that many film badges.
25. Richard Hallen: Can't remember even if I had a film badge for the one and only time I went into the bomb area.
26. R. Duane Kraft: I dispatched at the "HOT MOTOR POOL" location at Control Point Site. Never was issued a film badge and the Vehicles were contaminated.
29. Floyd Brittenham: The records had to be corrected after the testing was done. They were not right. You could not get the same reading twice.
30. Richard Granger: Some men weren't issued film badges.
31. Melvin Whitehead: There wasn't enough film badges to go around.

41

34. Carl Lundgren: This was a new type of warfare. They didn't know the importance or impact of the film badge.

35. James Fosnaugh: Sometimes film badges were in short supply.

36. Paul Miller: The reason not everyone got a film badge was, lack of knowledge as to what radiation would do to your health later on in life.

37. Gus Garcia: To my knowledge it was not enforced. Some left badges at camp or just forgot them at the sites.

39. Paul Martin: All I remember is that a few of our guys remained behind a few days to work on correcting the film badge records.

42. Albert Parrish: Only on site field workers got film badges, and then only on specific times. And the records were mixed up by too many inexperienced men working on them.

43. John Slomba: I was given a film badge every time I went into the field. Then after a while they told me I could not go out in the field, because I had my limit.

QUESTIONNAIRE #II

NAME   **DATE:**

1. Did you work on decontaminating radiation in Nevada on the atomic bomb tests?

Yes <u>20</u>   No <u>14</u>   Didn't Know <u>2</u>

2. Did your protective clothing consist only of a pair of conventional everyday coveralls and cloth booties?

Yes <u>30</u>   No <u>1</u>   Didn't Know <u>5</u>

3. When you took off the coveralls, did you go back to your hut before removing your fatigues?

Yes <u>26</u>   No <u>4</u>   Didn't Know <u>6</u>

4. What other types of protective clothing were you issued?
ANSWERS ON SEPARATE PAGE

5. What was done to decontaminate vehicles? People?
ANSWERS ON SEPARATE PAGE

6. Do you think all of the radiation was removed when decontaminated?

Yes <u>0</u>   No <u>32</u>   Didn't Know <u>4</u>

7. Was the only thing used to decontaminate vehicles and people soap and water?

Yes <u>31</u>   No <u>2</u>   Didn't Know <u>3</u>

8. How much experience did you have in decontaminating radiation before you arrived at the test site?
ANSWER ON SEPARATE PAGE

9. Was your training in your opinion "on the job?"

Yes <u>29</u>   No <u>1</u>   Didn't Know <u>6</u>

10. Did you keep any contaminated clothes in your clothes bag at your hut?
Yes <u>22</u>   No <u>10</u> Didn't Know <u>4</u>

11. Were you ever allowed to wear a film badge in the camp (Mercury) where you lived?
Yes <u>1</u>   No <u>30</u> Didn't Know <u>5</u>

12. By today's standards do you think you were protected as good as you could have been?
Yes <u>0</u>   No <u>34</u> Didn't Know <u>2</u>

13. In your opinion was there ever any equipment put to use when it was too contaminated?
Yes <u>18</u>   No <u>3</u>   Didn't Know <u>15</u>

14. When vehicles were in short supply, were any ever ordered to be used out of the "Hot Yard" while the radiation level was too high on them?
Yes <u>13</u>   No <u>2</u>   Didn't Know <u>21</u>

15. When the radiation was removed from a vehicle, was the radiation that was removed taken away from the cleaning area?
Yes <u>1</u>   No <u>18</u> Didn't Know <u>17</u>

16. What happened to the radiation that was removed from clothing,vehicles and decontamination equipment?
ANSWER ON SEPARATE PAGE.

Questionnaire #2 - Question #4.

All original letters are on file with Albert G. Parrish.

Besides a pair of coveralls and cloth booties, what other types of protective clothing were you issued?

1.	Gerald Bacon	None
2.	Ernest Kommer	Coveralls and booties
3.	Raymond Hosfelt	None
4.	Hilmar Mayerhoffer	None
5.	Alan Daffer	Impregnated waxed cloth.
7.	Robert Johnston	None
8.	Bob Opseth	Don't remember
9.	Stephen Demel	Don't remember
10.	Richard Miller	None
11.	Ernest Trubl	No answer
12.	Joseph Slonka	We took them off, took a shower, and put on our army fatigues to go to our hut.
13.	Wally Hyser	None that I remember
14.	Larry Hibben	No answer
15.	Eugene Toronto	None
16.	Paul Martin	Face dust mask
17.	Don Arntz	None
18.	Minneapolis (unsigned)	Hats and gloves on decon station
19.	Gerald Fisher	Coveralls, rubber boots, gloves, but not forced to use
20.	Roy Bracht	None
21.	Norman Reiser	None
22.	Herbert Hong	None
23.	Richard Hallen	Don't remember any

	other gear.
24. R. Duane Kraft	None
25. Charles Huffman	None
26. Floyd Brittenham	We wrapped tape over our shoes
27. Richard Granger	No answer
28. Melvin Whitehead	Didn't have any protective clothing
29. Unsigned	Maybe gloves
30. Roman Mamer	None
31. Paul Martin	No answer
32. Leslie Full	Cap and mask
33. Orville Huffman	None
34. Larry Heintzman	No answer
35. Albert Parrish	None
36. Elmer Floback	None

Questionnaire #2 Question #5

All original letters on file with Albert G. Parrish.

What was done to decontaminate vehicles?   People?

1.	Gerald Bacon:	None
2.	Ernie Kommer:	No Answer
3.	Raymond Hosfelt:	Showers
4.	Hilmar Mayerhoffer:	Wash all around top and bottom, pluck stones from tires
5.	Alan Daffer:	Vehicles washed, people showered
6.	Robert Johnston:	We used steam and soap to wash off radiation
7.	Martin Grimes:	Wash vehicles and the people took showers
8.	Bob Opseth:	Vehicles were washed down with water. People I don't recall anything.
9.	Stephen Demel:	They were washed
10.	Richard Miller:	Nothing
11.	Ernest Trubl:	No Answer
12.	Joseph Slonka:	Really can't say.
13.	Wally Hyser:	Vehicles were washed, I don't remember changing clothes after being out in the field
14.	Larry I-Hibben:	Checked for radiation and personnel was sent to shower if contaminated. Maybe 2 or 3 times. Civilians

	sometimes had to leave clothes.
15. Eugene Toronto:	Water only, personnel stayed with vehicles all day, as they. came in from field.
16. Paul Martin:	Truck was parked somewhere, as it was very contaminated.
17. Don Arntz:	People took showers
18. Minneapolis (unsigned):	Wash, shower. Soap and water.
19. Gerald Fisher:	Washed with soap and water under pressure.
20. Roy Bracht:	I just helped and people just took showers.
21. Norman Reiser:	Vehicles washed with tide soap. People showered.
22. Herbert Hong:	No answer
23. Richard Hallen:	Don't know about vehicles, the only. thing I remember being done was to remove coveralls and booties.
24. R. Duane Kraft:	Sometimes vehicles were washed, sometimes contaminated vehicles were put direct in the hot pool.
25. Charles Huffman:	No answer
26. Floyd Brittenham:	Vehicles were sprayed with chlorine spray mixed by the guys and later just soap and

	water.
28. Melvin White:	Soap and water
31. Paul Martin:	Vehicles were sprayed with water. People showered.
32. Leslie Full:	Washed with steam cleaner w/bleach & danc.
33. Orville Huffman:	No answer
34. Larry Heintzman:	No answer
35. Albert Parrish:	Washed vehicles with tide soap and water. People coming off test site showered and put on dirty clothes. The only place I showered was back at Camp Mercury.
36. Elmer Floback:	Hosed down and took showers.

All original letters are on file with Albert G. Parrish.

How much experience did you have decontaminating radiation before you arrived at the test site? Years _____ Months _____Days_____

1.	Gerald Bacon	No answer
2.	Ernest Kommer	No answer
3.	Raymond Hosfelt	None
4.	Hilmar Mayerhoffer	None
5.	Alan Daffer	None
7.	Robert Johnston	None
g.	Bob Opseth	None
9.	Stephen Demel	None
10.	Richard Miller	None
11.	Ernest Trubl	No answer
12.	Joseph Slonka	No answer
13.	Wally Hyser	Not that I remember
14.	Larry Hibben	Month
15.	Eugene Toronto	None
16.	Paul Marlin	None
17.	Don Arntz	1 day
18.	Minneapolis (unsigned)	None
19.	Gerald Fisher	I day, limited
20.	Roy Bracht	None
21.	Norman Reiser	None
22.	Herbert Hong	None
23.	Richard Hallen	None
24.	R. Duane Kraft	None
25.	Charles Huffman	None.
26.	Floyd Brittenham	2 days
27.	Richard Granger	None
28.	Melvin Whitehead	None
29.	Unsigned	None

30. Roman Mamer	None
31. Paul Martin	None
32. Leslie Full	None
33. Orville Huffman	No answer
34. Larry Heintzman	None
35. Albert Parrish	None
36. Elmer Floback	None

Questionnaire #2 Question #16

All original letters on file with Albert G. Parrish

What happened to the radiation that was removed from clothing, vehicles, and decontamination equipment?

1.	Gerald Bacon:	Watered down, went on ground
2.	Ernest Kommer:	I do not know
3.	Raymond Hosfelt:	I don't know
4.	Hilmar Mayerhoffer:	I worked only 1 day on decontamination
5.	Alan Daffer:	Drained down over bank & exposed to sun & air.
7.	Robert Johnston:	As far as I can remember, it was washed down the drain. (people) and down the driveway (vehicles
8.	Bob Opseth:	Don't know
9.	Stephen Demel:	Don't know
10.	Richard Miller:	Don't know
11.	Ernest Trubl:	No answer
12.	Joseph Slonka:	I really can't say
13.	Wally Hyser:	Don't know
14.	Larry Hibben:	Stayed at the site until it dissipated.
15.	Eugene Toronto:	It was just a run off down the drain. Into the sand in the test area.
16.	Paul Martin:	No answer
17.	Don Arntz:	Down the floor drain with people
18.	Minneapolis (unsigned):	I don't know
19.	Gerald Fisher:	Water from washing vehicle I believe was washed down a drain. Clothing issued was

	returned to CP..however, in some cases personnel not washing vehicles were in the area with regular clothes.
20. Roy Bracht:	Where we washed clothes, it went down the drain.
21. Norman Reiser:	I don't know
22. Herbert Hong:	Don't know
23. Richard Hallen:	Don't know
24. R. Duane Kraft:	Don't know
25. Charles Huffman:	Don't know
26. Floyd Brittenham:	When I worked the decontamination place it was left on the ground from the Vehicles I don't know about clothing.
27. Richard Granger:	Vehicles were done outdoors and went on the ground. Showers for the men went down the drain.
28. Melvin Whitehead:	Don't know
29. Unsigned:	It was hosed off the cement area, but I don't recall if there were any drains in the area.
30. Roman Mamer:	No answer
31. Paul Martin:	No answer
32. Leslie Full:	Went down a drain
33. Orville Huffman:	No answer
34. Larry Heintzman:	No answer
35. Albert Parrish:	It ran off the pad and soaked in the ground.
36. Elmer Floback:	Don't know

Dear Mom and Kate: 25 April 1952

Well, I'll try to get a little writing done cause I got the day off today. It's 10:00 o'clock in the morning Sat... I'll be back in Denver by the 15th of June if they don't send me to the Islands for Atomic tests. We have had 3 drops so far and we've been here 6 weeks tomorrow, but they are going to come fast from now on. I can't tell you how many is left, so I guess I won't talk about that. I can tell you the living conditions though. I live in a hut with 4 others. Their names are Sgt. Laudie, Me, P.F.C. Huffman, P.F.C. Szille, and P.F.C. Oberle. So there are 5 of us in here. The walls are made of plywood with now windows, and they have no roofing on them. Just a plywood roof. So it doesn't keep anything out. Dust, Rain, Snow, Gravel, or anything else makes it's Home in the huts.

It is swept out every morning, and right after it's swept you can't step on the floor barefoot or your foot is black. There is no way of mopping it cause the water out here costs the Army $.07 a gallon. So they really frown on, what they call excess use of water. We pay $.50 a night to sleep here, and $1.00 a meal to eat. You just pay a dollar when you come in and eat till you want to go out. It's really exceptionally good too. The Army don't have anything to do with the chow. The Civilians are really good, I'm getting a little fat out here on it.

Every one that reads the paper knows more about what we're doing than we do. They ask a million questions, but we just don't know the answers. I have been stationed on one shot right at the same base that Merv. trained at for two days. I've been in and out of there a dozen times on business, so I know pretty well what kind of camp Merv. was stationed at. The camp is 9 miles out of Vegas. Our camp is 65 or 70 miles North of Vegas. Mercury is the second largest populated area in Nevada. Reno and Las Vegas are the biggest. Mercury has about 4 or 5 thousand men. They are all working for the A.E.C. Nevada is about 75% desert and 25% Mountains. There is only about 150,000 population for the whole state. That ain't as much as St.

Louis Park is it?? At one time it was a pretty rich mining state, but they have drained it and moved out, so there is nothing but desert left.

Smoky

33

   This is a letter I wrote home to my mother and sister, while I was stationed in Mercury, Nevada, in 1952. If you look at the picture of the Hut you will notice the plywood window covers, propped up with a board. There was no glass, just screen under the covers. This way, if we propped-up the window covers we could get a little breeze through the Hut.

   If you read the letter you will see that water was costing $.07 per gallon, or as much as gasoline, so the A.E.C. wouldn't allow us to wash or scrub our Huts out. They called that a waste of water. Our wages were, for a Private, $75.00 per month.

   On page 10 of report # DNA 6019F : This is a location map of the 8 shots. You will notice that the very first shot (Able) was less than 10 miles from Camp Mercury, where we lived. The other seven shots were over 40 miles away from our camp. We lived in these huts for the rest of the tests, (91 days). The A.E.C.'s judgment was poor.. This shot near our camp should have been the last one, because every day we had to pass less than three miles from that Ground Zero, going from camp to work, and when we came home at night. We never were allowed to carry film badges from the Control Point to the Camp. I'm sure we had a lot of unrecorded radiation while going to work and back.

In our huts we had 5 Army cots, a 100 watt light bulb, and an oil burner. With the wind blowing in the desert, even with the shutters closed, with nothing but a plywood roof, sometimes when we woke up there would be a quarter of an inch of dust and radiation on your bunk.

We were dedicated to do the best job we could for our country, so we did not complain, after all, we heard some of the Desert Rock troops were sleeping in tents.

We knew the consequences, and it was a race between Russia and the United States. If Russia would get their Atom Bomb perfected before the United States, their intentions were to annihilate America. There were only four nuclear tests by America, before Russia detonated their own, first atomic bomb on August 9, 1949.

The real "Pioneers of Nuclear testing of the Atom Bomb", were The 216th Chemical Service Company, in the Tumbler-Snapper Atomic Tests in April through June 1952.

The first Nuclear bomb tested in the United States was July 16,1945, At Alamagordo, New Mexico, just 3 weeks before bombing Hiroshima, Japan.

The second Nuclear bomb tested in the United States was at Nevada Test Site, on January 27th, 1951. This was just 14 months and 4 days before the Tumbler-Snapper tests, that we were a part of, started.

This following paragraph is taken from "THE FORGOTTEN 216TH" newsletter, dated May 1, 1997. You will find that every Veteran who has been in the Atomic Tests, whether in Nevada,. in the Pacific Ocean, or any other place, and as far as that goes any school child know that this type of research is not accurate.

I cannot understand how the U.S. Government spends so many millions of dollars on a "SCIENTIFIC INDIVIDUAL RECONSTRUCTION OF RADIATION DOSAGE STUDY." That is absolutely A JOKE.

To say that 2 people work in the same Nuclear Plant so both people should have tile same radiation exposure. Then I have to ask,. why not just issue one film badge, to only one employee on each shift in the nuclear plant?. I think throwing darts at a given target would be more accurate than this so-called scientific way it is being handled by our Government.

The 39 men listed below have individual letters written in this book. You will understand, alter reading these letters and this book that this following paragraph is correct in all respects.

"THE FORGOTTEN 216TH" Newsletter

"Some of our members have asked the Government for their individual radiation exposure numbers, only to be told that because of lost records in a fire in St. Louis, or other dodges, that they can only offer a reconstructed exposure, based on where you might have been in relation to some other individual or group whose exposure is probably also incorrect. We find this to be unacceptable. We fed that these reconstructions are deliberately and artificially made lower than the true exposure."

57

Please read the following letters written by 40 men from different parts of the United States, all at the same time, about their jobs and experiences while serving in the Tumbler-Snapper, or (T.S.) tests of the Atomic Bombs. THESE ARE THE FACTS.

Stan Johnson	R. Duane Kraft	Glen Wells
Ardeen Zierott	Wally Holland	Albert Parrish
Dick Granger	Roy H. Bracht	Victor Oberle
Roman Mamer	Richard Hallen	Gerald Fisher
Norman Reiser	Don Arntz	Robert K. Arnett
Leslie Full	Charles Jameson	Walter Hyser
Charles Huffman	Warren Slavicek	Dick True
Ronald Brower	Franklin Duester	Melvin Whitehead
Roy Bushby	Carl Lindgren	James Fosnaugh
Paul A. Martin	Paul L. Martin	Orville Huffman
Larry Hibben	Bob Opseth	Stephen Demel
Ralph Thomas	Gus Garcia	Joseph Slonka
Gene Toronto	Hilmer Mayerhoffer	Herb Hong
	Gerald Bacon	

THE 216TH CHEMICAL SERVICE COMPANY IN OPERATION TUMBLER/SNAPPER 1952

When evaluating the use of film badges please consider these points:

1) The 216th was 90% of the AFSWP Radiation Safety Group.

2) The average age of 134 216th members was 22.

3) President Truman authorized these tests in January 1952 and 60 days later the 216th was at the tests as an integral part of the safety program.

4) In order to get the tests under way we were told we would be perfectly safe. We did not have the opportunity to volunteer even though it should have been a volunteer situation with full disclosure of the dangers.

5) Until we arrived at Mercury, Nevada we did not know what a film badge was and we were expected to become safety experts in their use.

6) Our training consisted of 2 weeks of rote instruction which is--do this--and so on without any training toward an in-depth understanding of radiation or its effects on human biology.

7) As the AFSWP Radiation Safety Group we were responsible for the radiation safety of everyone else through monitoring with Geiger Counters and developing and reading film badges and dosimeters. We were like the blind leading the blind.

8) Most of the people who ran the program were as inexperienced as we were.

9) The calibration of the densitometers used to read the film badges was set by a young man exposing new, unused film badges to a piece of radioactive cobalt right in an open area of the command post where anyone could watch.

10) The exposed film badges were developed in a darkroom sink where they were subject to problems such as temperature and chemistry variations and unsophisticated timing with a simple Gray-Lab timer.

11) The developed badges were read by minimally trained people using densitometers measuring exposure density in decimals of roentgens.

12) There was often incidental radiation from fallout particles on collection filters, film badges, and on the clothes of people who had been exposed and even on the people themselves. If you were not going out in the field you had no badge to check. If you handled anything with your bare hands, exposure could be localized.

13) Avoiding exposure at all times was never emphasized.

My conclusion, through my experience and 40+ years of hindsight, is that film badges were a low-tech answer to a very important and serious safety consideration.

Today the government uses the film badge findings as a convenient answer to criticism from people who believe-rightly so, in my opinion-that radiation has damaged them and their progeny. The government's view is obviously flawed.

If uncontrolled ionizing radiation is not damaging, why is there such emphasis today on limiting x-rays by doctors and dentists?

STANLEY L. JOHNSON
US 55 038 005

WHAT WE DID IN THE ATOM BOMB TESTS IN MERCURY NEVADA

This is a statement of my experience with, and opinion of, film badges used to measure ionizing radiation at the Tumbler/Snapper atom bomb test series in 1952.

I was a member of the 216th Chemical Service Company, U.S. Army Chemical Corps. Part of this company was sent to Mercury, Nevada in March 1952. We were 134 men and 4 officers. Recently I found out we were officially referred to as the AFSWP Radiation Safety Group.

Most of the 216th did radiation monitoring and were exposed to dangerous amounts of radiation in the field. We were told by "authoritative sources" that it would be safe and we had nothing to be concerned about The potential effects of relatively minor radiation exposure was never mentioned. I would like to believe that those in charge of the tests were truly ignorant, but in recent years I have decided they were more likely callous, devious and indifferent to the potential danger.

My job in the 216th was company photographer, so at the tests I was assigned to the photo lab where my only job was developing film badges after they were used in the field by the people exposed. When I say people exposed, I should include everyone at the Nevada Proving Grounds. For example-I was on a bus returning to Mercury from the Command Post through an area which should not have been "hot," but we had to leave the bus because it was "hot." I mention this because at these times there were no film badges to measure an individual's exposure.

Before I got to Nevada I had no idea what a film badge was. I found out it was similar to a dental x-ray film. The main difference was a small strip of thin lead wrapped around one end to create 1/2 inch clear film on the developed badge. In other words, the lead would protect this area from radiation exposure. The wrapper on each film had an embossed serial number which would later be used to identify, the person it was assigned to. The badge was clipped to the user in the chest area.

Whenever a new batch of badges with a different emulsion was opened for use, one of the Pad-Safe group would set up a 4 x 10 table on which there were clips to which new badges were attached at different distances from a known source of radioactive cobalt at one end of the table. I am not sure of how this exposure was formulated, but the results of this exposure was used to calibrate the densitometers to read the density of the blackness of the film badges. The blacker the badge, tile more radiation received. The clear area on the badge where the lead covered it was used to zero-in the densitometer.

After exposure, file badges were unwrapped in the darkroom and placed into sectioned trays similar to ice-cub trays with one badge to a section. There was a metal handle secured to the ends of the trays so they could be hung from an arm over a three-section sink, specially designed for developing these badges. I was told that the sink was temperature-controlled, but I cant say for sure that it was accurate.

The trays of films were developed one at a time by hanging them on an arm which moved up and down as it agitated the trays in each solution. Each step was timed by an ordinary Gray-Lab timer which was hand-set like an alarm clock. First, I positioned the arm over the developer and when the dock went off, I moved the arm over the hypo stop bath and reset the clock, then over the wash. The trays were then placed in a small heated dryer and given to the people who would take the densitometer readings. As I stated earlier, the badges were numbered and assigned to the users. The readers listed the density in decimal measures of roentgens after each name.

This system was not very sophisticated for such an important endeavor.

For one fixing, it relied on barely-trained young people who never realized how important it was to avoid radiation at all times. If everyone had known the dangers, the tests may never have taken place. At the very least, if the authorities knew the dangers, it should have been volunteers only. With 40+ years of hindsight, I believe that those in charge <u>did</u> know the dangers, but used those of us, who <u>did not</u> know, as physical and psychological experiments.

For another thing, there was always room for error during development such as: wrong temperature, errors in timing, bad chemistry, and the misreading of the badges.

And finally, remember that the vast majority of the AFSWP Radiation Safety Group were 216th members whose average age was 22 and what training we received in radiation monitoring was taught by rote. The Government Fact Sheets I have seen recently bear me out on how little training we had for a job that was so very vital to the physical well-being of not only our group, but of all participants in Operation Tumbler/Snapper. They show that we had only two weeks to learn what was expected of us. It was on-the-job training. I understand in later tests the military created a radiological safety specialist who was given a year of training.

TO SUMMARIZE:

I feel that all participants in Operation Tumbler/Snapper were involuntarily used to do what the government felt was necessary., without regard for future consequences.

Based on my experiences I feel that using film badges as a final opinion of radiation exposure is unrealistic. Everyday, while at the tests, most of the AFSWP Rad-Safe members had no badges.

Overall, I feel that not enough emphasis was put on these dangers of exposure. Based on the radiation safety precautions used today by doctors and dentists, I must be fight in my assumptions.

In Fact Sheets I have read recently, the government, conveniently, puts too much faith in film badges which give a flawed and inaccurate picture of the way things were. This is my opinion based on my experiences.

STANLEY L. JOHNSON
US 55 038 005

I was assigned to the 216th Motor Pool. My duties consisted of operation of a repair facility at the plants area of R.M.A., and other duties of acting Motor Sgt.

In mid March 1952 the 216th Chemical Service Company was assigned to participate in Operation Tumbler Snapper at Nevada test site. We were quartered in Mercury, Nevada and were given the duty of radiation monitoring in connection with the series of atomic tests of "Tumbler-Snapper." I was given the duty of operation of a "Hot Motor Pool" at the Control Point Site, and at other times was assigned monitoring duties along the test site perimeters. I do not remember the number of devices detonated. There were tower shots and air shots. I watched all shots from the A.E.C. (Atomic Energy Commission) Control Point using the 2.3 density goggles. Only on monitoring was I issued film badges or dosimeters. During the times of dispatching of the Hot Motor Pool I did not receive them. The vehicles assigned to the Hot Motor Pool were driven out into the desert test site areas and were used for radiation monitoring. To my knowledge they were not decontaminated In mid June of 1952, most of the 216th were returned to R.M.A. at Denver, Co.

I would sometimes have to work on some of the vehicles to make them ready to go out. so without a film badge at the Hot Motor Pool I know I received unknown radiation.

R. DUANE KRAFT
US 55 056 097

On the 25th of May 1952 1 watched the detonation, with my back to it until after the flash, and until I felt the heat on the back of my neck. After a short while my partner and I were sent to Groom Mine to evacuate it. There were 2 brothers owned the lead mine about 30 miles north and east of Ground Zero. We knew them well, we had visited with them when we had crossed the desert many times prior to this shot. It saved us 150-200 miles going to Caliente, NV and St. George, UT.

We got to the mine sad talked with the two brothers telling them to go to Las Vegas with their families and workers, and when they got there to call Control Point and the Government would pay all of their expenses until they could return and that may be a month or even several months.

I was in the kitchen with my back against file sink counter while file owners were carrying out their suitcases loading some of them in their small plane. I took a glass from the cupboard and drew a glass of water and drank it. I was just setting the glass down when one of the brothers came through carrying a suitcase and said, "You didn't drink the water, did you?" I said, "Yes. why?" He said, "You shouldn't have done that. Every time we get a shot coming this way we have to clean our water tank. It is above our house, and it has an open top."

I drew some water in my hand there was little black specks in it. So I went out to our vehicle and got the Geiger Counter, came back in drew some more water in my hand, and sure enough it Ws extremely hot with radiation. I told the officers about it when I got back to camp, but they just said, "Forget it, it won't hurt you." So I did forget about it at the time, not realizing there would be consequences most of my life."

Shot (Fox) was a shot on a 300 ft. tower. When the shot went off the steel tower disintegrated. The heat is so great that the rising of the heat .so fast sucks all of the dust and dirt and even the steel particles from the tower up into the mushroom and is carried with the high winds in any direction until the heavy, material (sand, dirt, steel, etc.) drops out. I guess that's why they call it "fallout." By the way, these 4 towers on our tests were 300 ft. or 30 stories high. The legs of the tower were 1" thick, 12 x 12 steel angle iron.

To show how poorly this testing was handled, this same shot (Fox) was scheduled for the 13 of .May and had to be postponed twelve days because someone forgot to hook the wires up at the bomb. Two civilians took several days walking 3-4 miles pulling the wires out of the ground trying to find a problem. The A.E.C. also thought that a relay was stuck and the bomb may detonate with the wind. We had to be there for the next few days prepared to go on a moment's notice. Adverse weather would only hold us up a day or two. I cannot imagine anything as deadly or dangerous as an atomic bomb without BACKUP SAFETY CHECKS. <u>CARELESS.</u>

ALBERT G. (SMOKY) PARRISH
US 55 038 034

Hi Al, I have avoided writing any letter on the subject of our duties at Camp Mercury, Nev. back in the early '50s.

My memory is so H.S. that I'm embarrassed to talk about what I did. I know I promised that I would write my recollections <u>I should have more info on the records than anyone.</u>

To the best of my recollection:

I departed Rocky Mountain Arsenal on Mar. 1, 1952 with 1st Sgt. David Lape and one other (Bud Floback?) on commercial airline for Las Vegas. I'm sure of this as it was my very first airplane ride. We were bunked in air-conditioned dom. Until the rest of you guys arrived some weeks later. We then moved into the infamous chicken coupes.

Our duties were to work at the Command Post (C.P.) between Yucca and Frenchman Flats. Part of the time prior to the arrival of the main body of people, was to pull guard duty out in middle of Yucca Flats. During the testing phase of <u>T</u>umbler/<u>S</u>napper (have to say that we always thought that meant

T.S. for Tough Shit), I believe my job was to record the radiation levels of peoples coming in from the field.

One pretty good recollection, is that I was commandeered on the last test shot, to go into the field to monitor the radiation by following the marked 2x4's that were placed at 100 yard intervals in Octagonal lines meeting at Ground Zero. You can check with Larry Hibben. He was the rider with me. (I was an unauthorized driver, having failed the drivers test given to me the day prior to the last shot) Isn't that funny that I would remember that.

But the most important fact is..I was commandeered because there were no bodys left who had not received the maximum allowed dosages. Sgt. David C. Lape (I think) told me to get my you know what over to the motor pool and get the drivers test so that we would have enough people to cover the measuring after the test. I returned to Rocky Mountain Arsenal just after the last test and prior to the main body. of troops leaving Camp Mercury. My job after returning was to prepare the necessary papers to pay. TDY per diem for all 216th troops. I returned to RMA with Sgt. Lape and 1 other enlisted man--can't remember who.

If you guys recall, the Government called us together (either at Camp Mercury or back at Rocky Mountain Arsenal) and asked us to extend our time of active duty by 3 months so that we could go to the South Pacific to monitor the H-Bomb tests. They then found out that we all received maximum radiation dosages and therefore the offer was withdrawn. (Do I have that correct?

WALLY HOLLAND
US 55 037 979

I was really not connected to any motor pool vehicles, I was a soldier who had to go in trenches dug in the ground about three miles from Ground Zero, and we who were there all had film badges. We all had our rifles and canteens and regular army clothes and helmets and were to watch the explosion and try not to effect our eyes because it was so bright. We did see the cloud form after the explosion. We even saw the airplane that dropped the so called "bomb."

I never did know what our film badges read.

ARDEEN ZIEROTT
US 55 076 214

I worked on film badges some, maybe I can help a bit. I know the monitor readers got a film badge and drivers also, to go out and read the radiation lines right after the blest then we got them to recover dropped projects. ' -

If I remember we just issued at the C.P. office. I think name, rank, and serial no. so they could be easily identified. When they were turned back in we read and recorded them, put the badges under a deal and it told us what the radiation reading was. I worked in that office twice while in Nevada, then Commander Bussey either took or mailed them to Washington.

Sam Johnson, Cleon Carpenter, Reed Kendall, myself, and a young fellow with the 216th I cannot recall his name, stayed behind and redone the records as they were screwed up.

We were not trained to handle film badges at all. It was on the job training and some people were damn poor record keepers. Putting any film badge in any envelope. That's why we stayed behind, 4 of us and redone the records. They were as up to date as could be when they left Camp Mercury. And like I said Col. Bussey either sent or delivered them to Washington, D.C., Pentagon I expect.

I also was on one of those deals, record radiation lines and get back to camp or C.P. I think we were supposed to go the 1-R line and turn back. And we did wear our regular fatigues back to our living quarters and left or wore them till we washed our clothes.

I do believe the A.E.C. could of done a lot better than they did. I think our 216th did as best we could at the time.

ROY H. BRACHT
US 55 038 057

I was with the 216th Chemical Corp that spent 3 months on the Atomic Testing grounds in Camp Mercury, Nevada in 1952 monitoring eight atomic bomb blasts. My job was driving a Jeep to the bomb site with another serviceman monitoring the radiation and all the contaminated equipment and contaminated animals that were brought into the Control Point.

We slept in plywood huts and wore the same clothes to our huts at night that we wore all day for the tests. We wore protective clothing (regular coveralls) over regular clothes but when we took them off at the control area, there was contamination all around the area.

The Jeep I was driving got high centered about 100 yards from a blasting tower and was stuck for at least 30 minutes. We did not suspect that we were being used as guinea pigs.

In 1975, I started having thyroid problems and have been on medication ever since. The doctor said the sores on my face, arms, and chest are possibly skin cancers.

VICTOR F. OBERLE
US 55 056 050

For the next two shots, we moved to Groom and Lincoln Mine and stationed fallout trays and air samplers that were picked up by helicopter after the shot. I found out later that the area was closed. The water supply had an open top and we had been drinking contaminated water.

For the next shot I was assigned to the motor pool washing the trucks and Jeeps down after they had gone into the radiation zone. Some of the vehicles would not come clean and were held in a special area of the motor pool. I did notice, however, that if we ran short of vehicles the contaminated ones were put back into use.

RICHARD GRANGER
US 55 037 986

Once in Nevada, I can remember only going out to the bomb site area one time to monitor radiation levels. This was at least one day after the detonation at that sight so the only dust we encountered was what we stirred up ourselves. On this assignment, I was sent out with a Naval officer whose rank insignia was an oak leaf so he had to comparable in rank to an Army Lt. Colonel or full Colonel Rank is not important except that obviously, I (a lowly corporal) was sent to drive and to assist The vehicle was similar to a Jeep only a bit larger, perhaps a four-by of some sort. (Now, you would think that going into a hot area, they would want expert drivers.) <u>This was the first time I had ever driven a military vehicle</u>. We were assigned to drive along two grid lines toward Ground Zero making radiological measurements along the way until we reached a point where the reading was 10 roentgens per hour. There we planted a flag, made a "U" turn and got the hell out of there. During one of these "U" turns, I killed the engine for just a moment. The only thing I remember was that the Naval officers face turned red and his eyes got big as saucers. Obviously he knew more about radiation than I did. After returning the vehicle to the decontamination point, I can remember that we took off our coveralls and booties and tossed them in a pile-I can't remember anything about the decontamination of the vehicle or of ourselves. I think we had film badges but I don't know for sure. Underneath, I was wearing my fatigues which I'm sure I wore back to the contractor hut I was staying in. I don't know for sure but I probably wore those same fatigues for the next day or two before tossing them in the laundry bag.

From this experience, I can say that prior to going into the hot zone, I should have had more experience driving the vehicle.

70

On returning from the hot zone, I don't believe we, meaning our bodies, were properly decontaminated. (We should have had showers and a complete change of clothing.)

RICHARD C. HALLEN
US 55 037 974

My duties consisted of <u>non commissioned officer in charge</u> of decontamination, and I assisted on a few grid line monitor assignments. The decontamination duties consisted of checking each vehicle returning from the actual area of detonation. Vehicles were washed and checked again, but most were placed in a "Hot Park." and used as needed. Everyone was exposed to the

"Hot" vehicles, and would drive them for further support missions regardless of degree of contamination. When we decontaminated these vehicles we were exposed to the contaminated water both by splashing and the drainage system. Many times my personnel and myself would be completely wet from the decontamination process. When personal film badges were turned in, some of them indicated (degree of cloudiness) exposure above that permitted, but nothing was done. '

The duties of a grid line monitor consisted of a driver and another individual whose job was to take readings and relay them to the Control Point. The team would depart file C.P. immediately after the initial flash and with the cloud raising. They would take their assigned grid line and begin calling back their readings, if a grid line ran though the projected fallout area, they would be subjected to high degrees of radiation. I can recall my driver and myself going through this experience and was concerned when our film badges were almost black. We were driving over fused sand (glass) a good deal of the time. We were again told not to worry. I was given a blood test monthly for 6 months, and results were never explained to me. I am not sure if others were given blood tests.

GERALD D. FISHER
RA 15 271 438

I was in the 216th Chemical Army Co. from 1950 to 1952. Our company helped test 8 nuclear bombs in Tumbler/Snapper Series (April through June 15). Some bombs were smaller, some much larger than used on Japan. All were above ground.

We were ordered to destroy all notes and forget everything because this was top secret. I remember sleeping in 5 man huts made out of plywood. Some mornings after a strong wind the dust and possible fallout would be 1/4 inch thick on everything (we were at Camp Mercury). Our huts were about 8 miles from the test site. We used no masks or protective clothing. We had film badges in the high radiation areas.

One day at Control Point while waiting for work orders (no film badges) someone went out with a Geiger Counter and found a high count. At that time we took cover.

I was a monitor testing radiation in the test area so I saw all 8 bombs explode. I also saw Marines and Army men come out of the trenches after detonation, also saw paratroopers jump in the area (after detonation).

In Nevada I worked in the blast area near the Marines as they came out after the blast. I also went in with scientists to pick up equipment on other tests. DNA says I received 1.399 roentgens of Gamma. Who knows how much alpha and beta particles we inhaled and ingested with all of the dust.

ROMAN MAMER
US 55 037 809

About ten days to two weeks before the rest of the 216th Chemical Company from Rocky Mountain Arsenal in Denver,

Colorado got orders to go to Camp Mercury, Nevada, a Lieutenant and about ten of us enlisted men were sent as an advance committee to the Atomic test site at Camp Mercury, Nev. They assigned five of us to each plywood constructed building they called huts. Then we paired off in pairs and were assigned Jeeps. We were sent to a controlled point which was I think about 20 miles from camp. The men and Jeeps were sent off in five different directions looking for radiation each day.

One of my partners (Ron Schuster) and I located a crater that we later found out that is where a underground Atomic bomb was set off a year or two before we arrived. There was a huge amount of radiation in this crater. (The first atomic bomb in the continental U.S. was detonated in Alamagordo, New Mexico 7-16-45. The second one was in Mercury, Nevada on 1-27-51, 14 months and 4 days before our first shot.)

I had several different jobs while at the command post, including some were, a partner and I would get in a Jeep after a bomb would go off and drive out towards Ground Zero and were told to stop when our Geiger counter reached and certain point and not let any G.I.'s or civilians go past that point. We had to stay there all day. There were several other guys doing the same thing. We had our film badges and docimeters on in order to see how much radiation we had picked up.

Our protective clothing consisted of a pair of coveralls and cloth booties. That's all I can remember we wore. I don't know how many times I went on those missions but it was more than once. We all had to report back to Controled Point after each mission. They checked our Jeeps and us for radiation. We turned in our film badges and decimeters. Then we took off our protective clothing, which was worn over our regular clothes, and we wore our regular clothes back to the huts.

I also read the film badges and decimeters on some days that; the atomic bombs were set off. These were very long days as we got up at 5:00 A.M. and didn't get to bed till after midnight or later. I recorded the film badges and decimeters on each G.I.'s card. The darker the film badge, the more radiation

73

the G.I. picked up. Two of these guys' docimeters were read as high as they would go and the film badge was completely black. I don't remember what the readings were. Later I found out these two guys were partners that day. One guy died shortly after we were discharged and the other one died but I don't know when. Every G.I.'s film badge that I read had picked up radiation. I don't know how much radiation I picked up but I was out in the field quite often. I feel that some of my physical problems are related to the radiation I had come in contact with while serving my country. If I knew then what I know now, I would have been more apprehensive about doing a job I was ordered to do.

DON ARNTZ
US 55 029 961

I was an off-site monitor on one shot. This means I was in a vehicle (Suburban) with a Geiger counter trying to locate the fallout from one of the atomic tests. There were approximately ten teams of two men to a team. My partner and I were to patrol in Death Valley and stay in contact with our radio with a C47 airplane that was flying overhead. We went out before daylight and all of the crews had strict orders, "Do not leave your vehicles until one of the crews locates the fallout." We had looked until one or two o'clock in the afternoon. No one had located the fallout yet and we got orders to leave Death Valley and patrol Highway 95 from Amargosa Valley to Goldfield. We were driving north on 95 and came to Beatty. We came to a restaurant, and we swung into the parking lot. One of us was going to stay with the vehicle as we were ordered, the other one was going to run in and get some sandwiches or something to eat. The probe was hanging out the fly window. When we drive up next to a parked car the Geiger counter went crazy. We had found hot radiation. I jumped out of the vehicle with the Geiger counter and it led me to the car. it was hotter by the back end of the car. I put the probe up under the left rear fend. That was the hottest spot. While I was bent over with my arm up under the fender, a couple of fellows from the restaurant seen me and thought I was stealing the tires. They came running out, and right up to us yelling at us. Then they seen <u>A.E.C.</u> on the back of our coveralls, and backed away from us. Then the lady that owned the car came out. We told her she had run through the fallout (radiation) and we wanted to know where she had been, so we could pinpoint the location. She started screaming because she though she was going to die. She was hysterical, but we found out that she had been down in Death Valley on some little out of the way side road. We radioed the location and the Control Point must have sent some one else in because we never went back into Death Valley on that shot.

When we got in that night we were called up to Headquarters and several of the officers wanted to courts martial both of us for telling the woman that she had radiation on her car, when we were caught in the act of locating what we were sent out to find. We were not on site so we did not have film badges.

I heard later that the Government had to settle financially, buy her a different car, and dig up her front yard where the car was parked for a while before coming to the restaurant.

On another shot we had air sampling stations set up at Currant, Ely and Warm Springs. On the day of the shot we would have to pick up filters and drive about 80 miles per hour to an abandoned Government airport south of Highway Six between Tonopah and Warm Springs. There we met an Army C47. They. would transport the filters back to the Control Point by air. We had to do this as fast and as many times as we could on shot day and sometimes for several days. The filters sat beside us on the seat on our runs. AGAIN, WE NEVER HAD FILM BADGES. We also were ignorant about the effects of radiation. We were lead to believe it was harmless.

ALBERT G. PARRISH
US 55 038 034

ASSIGNED JOBS:

1.   Onsight ground radiation monitoring into area of Ground Zero and surrounding area.
2.   Fly as radio operator on C47 (code name 747) to receive readings and information from our ground based monitors, then relay the information to the Control Point on site.
3.   Fly as monitor on L-20 De Haviland Beaver (code name Woodchuck #1 or #2). These flights were flown much as a spray plane would fly at very low altitude while I took radiation readings at assigned grid coordinates on the test site and surrounding areas.
4.   Setting up and operating sampling equipment at Indian Springs Air Force Base.

DESCRIPTION OF JOB PROCEDURES:
1.   When doing on-site monitoring on the ground I always wore protective clothing issued along with a film badge and dosimeter. Upon returning to the C.P. area from our mission we would get out of our protective clothing shower and check ourselves to make sure we were decontaminated. Was this the right procedure? I don't know.
2.   I flew as radiation operator on the C47 out of Indian Springs. We overflew the areas that ground based monitors were assigned in order to receive and relay their information to the Control Point. No protective clothing was worn and I do not remember film badges or dosimeters. No monitor equipment was carried on these flights.
3.   I flew as low altitude terrain survey monitor aboard the L20 aircraft on every test during operation Tumbler-Snapper. They had originally planned to have two monitors fly the missions in two aircraft, however after the first mission the other monitor quit due to the type of flying involved. They were to replace him with someone else but never did so I ended up flying the rest of the missions alone.

Everything went pretty much as planned except on shot George, June 1, 1952. As we would normally fly into Ground Zero we would start picking up higher radiation and would begin skirting around Ground Zero in order to keep the radiation to an acceptable level. For some reason it did not work out as normal on that particular date. We had two Geiger counters on board, one to read low level and background, the other to read high level radiation. Approaching Ground Zero we started picking up high amounts of radiation, much faster than normal and before I could tell the pilot my high range counter was pegged at top scale, which I remember to be 500 roentgens, so I have no idea just how hot the area was. As soon as we got through this area I advised the pilot that we should return directly to Indian Springs, as we had just clobbered the aircraft and we had to get out of it as soon as possible, which we did. We changed planes at Indian Springs, went back up and completed our mission. It took approximately seven days to decontaminate the aircraft before we could use it again. Neither the pilot nor I were wearing protective clothing and I do not recall film badges or dosimeters.

ROBERT K. ARNETT
US 55 056 055

On one occasion my partner and I were sent out to a certain grid on the proving ground map. We had a pair of coveralls on over our fatigues. This was our protective clothing. We were supposed to stay there for a certain number of hours and see how much radiation we would collect on our film badges. We were ordered not to sit under any trees. In other words, right out in the open (there were no trees in this part of the desert). My partner and I sat on the ground about 50 feet from the Jeep. It was terrible hot out there with the coveralls on, so for a while I got sick and layed down in the pick up truck, with both doors open. When we got back and had our film badges read, we wore called up by the officers in charge. They wanted to know why my film badge didn't read as high as my partner's read. The officers again threatened to courts martial us. They accused me of dropping my partner off and going somewhere else. I wouldn't dare tell them I was laying in the pick up, so I lied and my partner swore to the fact that I was sitting on the ground within 50 feet of him.

ALBERT G. PARRISH
US 55 038 034

Once I was at Las Vegas City, Building where the city kept their equipment, tractors, trucks. Then another time was Nellis Air Force Base. The one I really remember was the one I was Navy. Chief Warrant Officer. I don't remember names. We went to Death Valley Furnace Creek. Kept in touch with C47 airplane. We a Chev. Suburban which they new where we were all the time with our little Geiger counter and film badges.

Then another time went a ways out on the desert. They had a bunch of stuff, airplanes, Jeeps, trucks, and ail kinds of equipment, just to see what the blast would do to them. I guess. I don't remember how far from Ground Zero that was. Trucks and Jeeps were all blown apart Wheels and tires were not hurt. Tires still had air in them. Airplanes did not look like they were hurt except the windshields and side windows were all shattered where you couldn't see through them.

Another time we were out around Ground Zero. Radiation was really hot, like walking on melted sand, it would really creak when we walked on it. We lived in 5 man plywood shacks painted silver. We wore the white coveralls and a film badge. Then at the check point where they washed the trucks, trailers, and cars before they let them through. They had some decon trucks, I think they were ours. Everything was washed with Tide soap. We were all there but different crews.

NORMAN (PEE WEE)REISER
US 55 056 095

In Nevada I was one of the buys that went out right after the bombs were set off to see how much radiation there was at Ground Zero. I was in Nevada from Apr. 1, 195 to June 30, 1952. I think there was 10 or 11 blasts while we were there. The series of tests were called Tumbler-Snapper. I received a total of 4.879 roentgens of Gamma radiation. (Many medical problems are listed in the letter.)

CHARLES A. JAMESON
US 55 076 599

At Mercury, Nevada I was assigned to monitoring in the test area and checking contamination on vehicles, etc. As far as protective clothing, I don't remember if we had any. I'm quite sure when I went to monitor in the test area I just wore our regular fatigues.

We were housed in small plywood buildings which reminded me of a chicken house. There were 5 or 6 men in a hut and it was rather crude for living quarters. Our clothes were worn and washed as any work clothes would be. There was no special handling of our clothes if we had been out to the test area monitoring or doing something else. At the time we were there I remember hearing that we were 6 miles from Ground Zero (actually 6-8 miles from Ground Zero on Shot Abel, the first shot of our tests to our living quarters at Camp Mercury). This is referring to where we were living. I do not know if this is factual or not.

Did we get some radiation? We had to have. We had film badges but I don't recall ever being told how much. When we had to go to monitor the test area, you had to stay at your position to more or less guard the road so cars of workers or scientists wouldn't go beyond end that point because it was too hot with radiation. I don't remember how many hours we had to stay at our post but it seemed like it would have been a morning or afternoon. The vehicles that I used were Jeeps or 3/4 ton open Army trucks. I never had one that I drove all of the time.

WALTER N. HYSTER
US 55 037 984

During the atomic test shots, at times I was in the deep of it. I wore some protective clothing, dosimeter and film badge. They I had 3.7 exposure. 4 was considered too high. (See dosage at the end of this letter.) I think I was burned out at the decon station. We cleaned vehicles from the forward area with steam cleaner and bleach. We didn't wear any special clothing. When returning from the forward area, we passed through 3 rooms. First to strip clothes, second to shower, third you were instrument checked. If a reading was found you reshowered till no reading. I helped to calibrate instruments, MX-5, Cutie Pie, and others. Then you wore protective clothing. They had a measured off area for distance. In the center was a lead vault underground, with a radioactive capsule placed on the vault lid to calibrate with. This was at the Control Point. You couldn't go out to Ground Zero for 10 days to 2 weeks after the shot. Then it was still plenty hot. When I was on "off site monitoring" you didn't wear protective clothing.

They had a bunch for 5 & 7 man huts for the enlisted men (no water) and they had a large hut with stools and showers. At night you had to shake the sand from your bedding. Once when watching a shot from the Control Point, the shock wave and heat wave hit us. We were thrown back a good 10 feet, flat on our backs. Under the goggles the skin was white and the rest was burned beet red. Back in 1986 I received a letter from Department of Defense, regarding a research effort to determine radiation dosage of D.O.D. personnel in nuclear tests. The only reading they listed was for Tumbler-Snapper. Operation Dose 0.795.

LESLIE J. FULL
US 55 057 570

I was really over exposed once. As I recall it, was really drilled as to where I was. I've been in the hospital twice for breathing problems and they could find no cause. Also sinus, and my ears ring.

There were six straight lines out from Ground Zero, 3 to 4 miles long. One to two hours after the shot, 2 men to a Jeep would start from the outer Edge and go towards Ground Zero. There was a stake every 300 feet. At each stake a reading was taken and recorded. I can't remember if a reading was taken at Ground Zero. (It was 12 miles from Command Center to Ground Zero.) On return to Center, dispose coveralls to soil room, turn in film badge and dosimeter. Took a shower and dressed. Then it was my job to gather all 6 sheets and plot all the readings on a large wall map in Colonel Day's office. All my work was on the test site area. We bad 3 days on and 2 days off.

WARREN SLAVICEK
US 55 038 059

Hughes, John S. US 55 038 025: 216th Chemical Service Company, Death caused by radiation, wife compensated by the V.A.

Rogers, Douglas P. US 55 038 006: 216th Chemical Service Company,

Death caused by radiation, wife compensated by the V.A.

Tompkins, Patrick US 55 038 036: 216th Chemical Service Company,

Death caused by radiation, wife compensated by the V.A.

There have been many more deaths in our outfit from the after effects of radiation that I'm sure were turned away from

81

filing claims, while our medical records were sealed, calling them "top secret", for over 40 years. Only lack of funds keeps us from getting to the truth.

Much of the time I also spent at the decon station trying to get rid of high amounts of radiation from vehicles that had been taken down to Ground Zero or high radiation spots. If we could not clean up the radiation from the vehicle, we would then place this vehicle in the Hot Motor Pool and we try to wash this vehicle again later. Any amounts of radiation that we may have-picked up on our clothing which we then wore back to our huts, and was stored under our bed until the next time we did laundry.

Now here's a summary of what happened that day in 1952 when I got the major overdose. I say major, because there were other instances when we all were exposed one way or another, thirty minutes after a surface shot, four of us were sent to the blast site as an initial survey team to get as close to Ground Zero as possible using Geiger counters to measure the radiation levels. We were told to go as close as possible to a certain Geiger reading (I don't remember the number(and make notations. We were in an area where the dust hadn't settled, birds were fluttering, trying to fly but couldn't and were dying, and my badge changed complete color indicating over exposure. When we reported back to the Control Center (which if you recall was only seven miles from

Ground Zero) the officer in charge chewed our asses out because we got an overexposure and it would be inconvenient to send the required overdose report to Washington, D.C.

DICK TRUE
US 55 038 032

I was assigned to off-site operations. As I recall, I was issued film badges and dosimeters on two assignments to Groom Mine. The first time the dosimeter had a low range, possible background reading, with no way to read the film badge.

The second trip to Groom Mine, the dosimeter went off-scale, still no way to red the film badge; however, the detection instruments indicated that the "cloud and fallout" 'passed over my station. I had coveralls and booties taped on with masking tape.

CHARLES HUFFMAN
US 55 056 078

On one of the tests I was sent into Ground Zero two hours after the blast. I went in with a Geiger counter and took readings with another 216th Army man who was driving a Jeep. Don't remember who it was. It was in the middle of the program. We wore coveralls that were taped shut with masking tape and booties over our shoes. Wore dosimeter in our inside shirt pocket, which we turned in when we returned.

Turned in our coveralls and showered till we passed the Geiger counter readings.

One test guarded a pass into the test site with 2 A.E.C. guards. The fallout came our way and we had to go east to Highway 93 and back to Las Vegas to get back to Mercury and C.P. hail a Geiger counter with me but no protective clothing or badge.

One test I went with Seidel in a AEC pickup to Ely, Nevada to turn on a vacuum cleaner (tank type Electrolux) on the morning of the blast and then returned the filter to C.P. that same day. On tope of the tallest building. The rest of the time I was at the test site with a Geiger counter as a guard. I don't know what the reading was when I was at Ground Zero. Never informed what the reading was on the dosimeter.

FRANKLIN C. DUESTER
US 55 076 598

Went to Ground Zero 15 minutes after bomb went off. Had pocket dosimeter and film badge. Went to Groom and Lincoln

Mine for three days. Shortly after both mines were closed. The water tower reservoir was open on top and we had been drinking radioactive water. Also stationed at St. George Utah for one bomb. Then in the motor pool washing contaminated cars and Jeeps and putting them in hot parking or O.K. parking from radiation. Then went to personnel monitoring where men would come in and strip clothes and shower having to wash hair four to five times. The only time I had a pocket dosimeter and film badge was when I went to Ground Zero and back out again.

RICHARD K. GRANGER
US 55 037 986

When I was at Camp Mercury., Nevada once a week I checked permanent fallout stations. I handled contaminated filters with my bare hands. I didn't have any protective clothes, film badge or dosimeter. When I came back into camp I was never checked for radiation. I have had cancer of the pancreas.

MELVIN S. WHITEHEAD
US 55 076 621

Vehicles were hosed down. I did that at different times. I remember being out in the field with our Geiger counters, and one day stands out in my mind when I was ordered back to camp because I was told I had too much radiation. I don't remember any training for radiation effects and I don't think anyone else knew the danger of this material we used and handled, and if they did they did not inform us of such effects.

RONALD J. BROWER
US 55 057 549

Right after Charlie shot the Air Force Capt. asked me to take a party from the A.E.C. where he wanted to go. I assumed back to Camp Mercury. This started out at the Command Center about eight hours after the blast.

When I got to the vehicle I observed he was wearing protective gear. I turned toward Mercury and he said go the other way. I turned around and went as directed assuming he was going to the airfield. We proceeded towards the blast area and he asked me where my protective clothing was. I answered I didn't have any, he replied, then you'll have stay in the vehicle. We met Wally Mix and ?? by the trenches and were told to clear the area because it was too hot. He told them he was with the A.E.C. and was collecting samples of ground and I helped load them in the vehicle. Wind was blowing, I got sick and vomited. He drove back and two solders from 216th took me to barracks. I was sick for two days.

CARL W. LINDGREN
US55 037 981

As you know I was a member of the 216th Chemical Service Company and was one who took part in Operation Tumbler/Snapper. On one shot I was sent into the blast site with other members of the 216th, to get as close to Ground Zero as possible in order to get radiation reading. It was so hot our Geiger counter could not read the radiation. We were in the area where it was just like powder and the Jeep driver almost upset us all trying to get back out. My film badge indicating overexposure and when we returned back to the Control Center. I know the officer in charge really chewed asses because we got overexposure. I can remember being put in the shower for over one hour. trying to wash off the radiation. They tell me I only received 1.165 of radiation, but that is a bunch of bull.

I was one of the personnel left behind to clean up the mess, being assigned to help out in the film badge section. A Lt. Bussey, I think that was his name, made me help out in that section, but things were so screwed up it was impossible to put all the records in order. Some of them were kept in a book and numbers and were written after your name. Somehow the records seem to vanish. I worked very little on records. I spent over 6 months extra at Mercury, Nevada, and never once was I checked for radiation during all the extra time at the Control Point We wore no film badges and in my opinion we were just a bunch of guinea pigs for the U.S. Government. I came back to my company in Denver in February 1953 and was discharged in March 1953.

JAMES H. FOSNAUGH
US 52 142 694

One of my jobs was to help check vehicles coming back in from the fields that were contaminated. If we couldn't get a vehicle clean of contamination we would park it off to the side for 1-2 days and do it over again if the radiation wasn't down where we wanted it to be. They weren't always taken to another location right away where we washed them down.

The water just ran off the pad and soaked into the ground within 15-20 feet of where we played cards or checkers while waiting for another vehicle. We weren't always required to have coveralls on while waiting to do another vehicle.

I was also on off-site monitoring team. Went from town to town and other locations. One time I was being sent out to check an area for radiation with a fellow by the name of Oscar Hislaw. We had just gotten off post and our car quit. (We were betting our lives on these vehicles and equipment.) We called on the radio for someone to come pick us up. They took us to the motor pool for a different vehicle. We had our Geiger counters with us. When we went in the motor pool the Geiger counter went crazy. Some vehicles were still hot with radiation. Everybody. just laughed and they gave us another and away we went. If only somebody, really, cared, including me. I remember whoever give us instructions on how to read Geiger counters told us, "you could eat 10 M.R. of radiation and it wouldn't hurt you."

ROY BUSHBY
US 55 057 555

Our preparation and training was very. Brief--maybe 10 days. It took place at the test site when we arrived in Nevada, and as I recall, consisted mostly of how to work and read a Geiger counter. I was probably among the 45% of our group that was never issued a film badge. At least to my memory that was the case.

I worked in both on-site and off-site assignments, and in retrospect. I would say the decontamination procedures were very shoddy and careless. The off-site personnel, who followed the fallout, were never subjected to the decontamination process. In more recent years, as information concerning radiation and decontamination procedures used upon military personnel at the test site has come to light, I have become .convinced that were just a bunch of guinea pigs. I am constanty), amazed that our government has so little concern for file well-being of the military.

PAUL L. MARTIN
US 56 059 541

At Mercury, Nevada, I spent most of my tithe at the Command Post. My memory is not as good as I'd like it. So many fixings I've forgotten! I was usually on the radio, mapping out the fallout after a blast. I know the boys out in the vehicles did not realize the seriousness of what they were being asked to do. The officers in charge, I felt, did not fully understand either. To my knowledge, there was very little or no training before or during our stay at Mercury. At the time, I felt there was a great deal of carelessness in the way everything was handled. When there wasn't a fresh shot I was involved in passing out film badges to the civilians who worked out in the field. I don't remember ever wearing a film badge, even though contaminated vehicles, equipment, and clothing were always passing through the area.

ORVILLE B. HUFFMAN
US 55 057 558

WHAT HAPPENED ON JUNF. 5, 1952:

I and an Air Force sergeant were assigned the North and Northwest lines to read and radio back to the control point, the amount of radiation on (Shot How). We left about 6:00 A.M. and approached the South end of the North line of the shot. Our Geiger counter went up to 500 Roentgens, and all of a sudden the needle went past the 500 marker. We turned West and it came down so we proceeded towards the North to find our stakes on the Northwest line. As we came upon the stakes we turned on the radio to report in, and the radio was dead.

We went up a little further and the truck died. *(At this point two lives depended on this vehicle and/or this radio.)* I think we were getting a reading of about 20 roentgen. The Sergeant jumped out of the truck and said he was going to walk out (going North). I stayed with the truck and did not get down on the ground. I walked out on the hood and checked the engine over and worked on the wiring. By this time the Sergeant was about two blocks away. I got in the truck and it started. The Sergeant came running back and we went due East down the mountain to the highway, which was 2 or 3 miles away. I don't 'know the reading on the track but it was really hot with radiation. I worked in the film badge lab on reading film badges, so I know my reading was 3.52 and the Air Force Sergeants reading was over 6.5, but I don't remember his name.

In recent reports I see there are only two Air Force personnel with over 5.0 Roentgen, so he is one of them! Hope this tells you about the North and Northwest lines of Shot How and why they didn't hear from us. NOTICE FACT SHEET BELOW.

PAUL A. MARTIN
US 55 038 015

Quoted from Defense Nuclear Agency: Public Affairs Office, Washington,. D.C. "Fact Sheet" 14 June 1982
SUBJECT: Tumbler-Snapper: Page 5, Paragraph 5
Shot How was detonated from a 300-foot tower located in Area 2 of Yucca Flat, on June 5, 1952 at 03:55 hours. Show How, the last weapons test of Operation Tumbler-Snapper, had a .yield of 14 kilotons (equal to file same power as Hiroshima, Japan). No exercise desert rock program were conducted, but DOD personnel did participate in about 30 of the Test Group Projects. The on-site fallout pattern emended to the North and Northwest of Ground Zero, but the initial radiological survey team did not monitory that area because no recovery operations were necessary there. The survey team did measure intensities of 0.01 R/H as far as two kilometers to the West of Ground Zero."
Comment: The above is a cover-up on records to Washington, D.C. because they didn't get the measurements or radiation on North and Northwest lines. On the same page 5, Par. 6, "Most on-site and off-site radiological safety procedures were performed by the 'AFSWP' Radiological Safety Group, composed of personnel from Army, Navy, Air Force." This wasn't the only screw-up on this Shot How. On this same fact sheet Page 3, Paragraph 4, "Some of the paratroopers, however, jumped prematurely and missed the drop zone by as much as 13 kilometers (10 miles). Five paratroopers were slightly injured on landing." The records will show more injuries.

PAUL A. MARTIN
US 55 038 015

Although it is hard to remember everything from when I was in Nevada for the Atom Bomb tests, I can remember a few things. I recall being out at Ground Zero twice. There may have been another time also. the one time I was supposed to go out to Ground Zero shortly after the bomb had been exploded. I was supposed to go out and take readings with a Geiger counter at stakes in the ground. These stakes, if I remember correctly, were placed at 100 yard intervals, starting at 100 yards from Ground Zero. I was to take readings at every stake.

I don't remember how many there were supposed to be, but there were quite a few. I understood they wanted to see how the radiation dissipated as they got farther and farther from Ground Zero. When I got out there, I couldn't find any stakes at all. I guess they were just blown away or disintegrated by the blast.

I had a two-way radio in my Jeep. They kept in contact with me most of the time. When I told them I couldn't find any stakes, they told me to keep looking, which I did. Finally someone called me on the two-way radio and said it must be pretty hot out there. He was not referring to the temperature. He was referring to the radiation. I said it was. and I told him my Geiger counter wasn't much good to me became the radiation was so high that my Geiger counter was clear off scale. Shortly thereafter, he called back and said I'd better come in, which I did. The other time I went out I was in charge of a group of high level people, both military and civilian. I can't remember what kind of a vehicle I drove though. I was to act as their safety guide. I had a Geiger counter. I was supposed to be able to tell them where and how long they could stay.

One other thing I remember doing out there was checking cars, trucks, etc. at the gate as they left the large test area. At this gate, there was an A.E.C. (Atomic Energv Commission) guard with me. I had a Geiger counter and I would check ,all over the vehicles, especially the wheel area to see if there were any readings above the permissible levels. They told me I had complete authority at this gate to stop vehicles from leaving the test site if the radiation was above limits.

I did send quite a few cars, trucks, etc. back to be decontaminated because of too high radiation readings. Some didn't like it very well when I sent them back. In fact, some of them tried to get the A.E.C. guard to override me, but he told them he couldn't as I had complete authority on the radiation matter.

I know there is more, but this much I remember fairly clearly.

ROBERT B. OPSETH
US 55 037 975

In the middle of March 1952 1 was sent to Mercury. Nevada. We went out there in a truck convoy. I lived in a little wooden hut. There were 4 or 5 men in each hut. They would come out and pick us up with a bus in the morning and then bring us back at night. I worked in the supply room handing out supplies. Other times we did nothing. A truck would come up with food and we would get our meals from it.

I remember having to go out to the bomb site 2 or 3 times. We would put on coveralls when going out and carried instruments to read the radiation. I never did have to drive trucks. We were given special glasses to wear when they shot off the bombs. I was in Nevada until the middle of June 1952.

STEPHEN F. DEMEL
US 55 056 056

In 1952 I was a member of the 216th Chemical Service Company stationed on temporary. duty as part of the Radiation Safety Group at the Nevada Proving Grounds atomic test series-- Operation Tumbler/Snapper.

I was an Army private and had several different duties during the tests.

1) I drove a scientist into Ground Zero so he could check his equipment and collect data from his experiments. My main job

91

was to monitor radiation for our mutual safety. Needless to say, he was not very cooperative when I said we should leave so he put us both in danger of over exposure. I have since learned that no exposure is safe.

2) I also rode in a plane for cloud sampling and tracking to radio ground personnel about radioactive fallout.

3) Twice I went to Ground Zero shortly after blasts to check radiation levels. Once we got stuck in the sand in a high reading area and finally, after spinning our tires and stirring up much dust, we were about to get out, but only after several minuets of exposure.

4) Another time we were sent in to get radiation readings as close to Ground Zero as possible. We were in radio contact with the Control Center and they were trying to get a specific reading at a determined area, but we could not give them the info because we did not know exactly how close to Ground Zero we were. The stakes marking distances from the tower and the steel tower itself were evaporated and the surface sand was crystallized. Army tanks and airplanes being used for tests were melting or burning. The Control Center finally, asked us if the readings were high and we replied that our T1B Geiger counter which read 50,000 miliroentgens per hour was off scale and we were told to leave the area as quickly as possible. I guess we were in the high radiation area for 6 to 8 minutes.

5) I also worked in decontamination--detecting and removing radiation from personnel and equipment. We had to send some people back to the showers as many as 3 times to wash off the radioactive particles on their skin and in their hair.

6) I pulled guard duty with armed civilian security guards at a remote outpost road on day of shot to make sure no unauthorized people were in area of detonation.

LARRY HIBBEN
US 55 038 008

I received quite a lot of radiation. We carded dosage meters and checked the radiation until it reached 4000 Miliroentgens. We calibrated our instruments with a piece of Uranium on a post located in the center of 11 circles. The circles were 1 yard (36 inches) apart.

The Radium was so hot that it took 2 men to calibrate one instrument. One man stood outside the 33 foot circle a pen and tablet. He wrote down the readings as the man with the

Geiger counter would step on the 11 yard line and call the reading out, then step on the 10 yard line and call the reading out. The man with the instrument would call out the readings as fast as possible, until got to the one yard line (3 feet) from the-radium, then he was to run around and RUN back to the outside of 11 yard line. After one of the team was finished calibrating his own instrument, he would take the pen and pad, while the other teammate would call out his own Geiger counter readings to the one who had already finished calibrating his.

Stakes were driven and marked every 1/10th of a mile from Ground Zero out in 6 different directions for several miles before detonation of each bomb.

My job was to drive a vehicle with a partner after each bomb was detonated on one of the coordinates of the pie like lines up to the HOT readings near Ground Zero. We were to record and call in to the Control Point by radio the stake marking and the Geiger counter reading for that stake. The Control Point then mapped the radiation intensity around Ground Zero on a large map on the wall. We were to leave a flag and a sign at a given amount of radiation and no one was to go past that point, then we were immediately supposed to mm around and get out of the high amount of radiation to a safer area. We had a film badge and dosimeter (most of the time I remember)

On one bomb I was in a trench with other me. I had a film badge, dosimeter and a Geiger counter to take reading. We kept our heads down until after the detonation.

S/SGT GUS GARCIA

I'm sending you back this questionnaire with what all I know about the Tumbler-Snapper. It's been too many years to remember, so I did the best I could and answered all I could for you. You see I'm not in the best of health anymore. I've been in the hospital for open heart surgery, and everything seems to be falling apart on me that I'm getting older. I hope this helps.

JOSEPH J. SLONKA
US 52 111 066

I was stationed at Rock Mountain Arsenal for a total of two years with the exception of schooling for eight weeks at Fort Lee, Virginia and three months at Camp Mercury, Nevada.

While at Camp Mercury. (approximately March 1952 to June 1952) we were used as monitors to determine the amount of radiation in certain areas. To do this we would carry a Geiger counter to an area where lab personnel would need to retrieve what they had placed in that area before the bomb went off and if we entered an area where the radiation level was too high we would then back out and leave this site until a later time. In many cases there were high levels of radiation.

Much of the time I also spent at the decon station trying to get rid of high amounts of radiation from vehicles that had been taken down to Ground Zero or high radiation spots. If we could not clean up the radiation from this vehicle, we would then place it in the "hot" motor pool and we would try to wash this vehicle again later.

Any amount of radiation that we may have picked up on our clothing which we then wore back to our huts, was stored under our bed until the next time we did laundry.

In 1967 (11 years after I received my discharge) I had my first heart attack. 17 years later I had my next heart attack.

RALPH THOMAS
US 55 038 061

My duties at Mercury, Nevada during 8 atomic blasts were as follows: One three occasions I was an off-site monitor. On the first test I was at Glenwood Springs, Nevada. The second test I was at Alamo and Caliente, Nevada. The third time I was at Beatty and Indian Springs, Nevada.

I was an on-site monitor for 5 atomic tests. On these tests I operated a Geiger counter and checked to locate radiation. We checked for radiation levels up to 20 Roentgens. I received approximately 2900 Milliroentgens of radiation on my badge over a period of three months.

HILMAR A. MAYERHOFFER
US 55 038 060

We were sent to Yucca Flats in Nevada early in 1952. Our job was to monitor Atomic Radiation after each bomb was exploded. The job included chasing the fallout in and around the State of Nevada.

We were told to approach Ground Zero within a half hour of detonation. I would check a vehicle out of the motor pool and pick up another monitor. One time it was a Navy Chief.

With our Geiger counters we would spend most of the time monitoring radiation. We had almost no protective gear, no mask or outer gear, except for cotton coveralls. If we returned to the Command Post we would enter a recording room to see how much radiation we were exposed to. There was not much accuracy hear because they could not register the amount of radiation we ingested or inhaled while we were on the desert.

When we went from the test site back to our camp (Camp Mercury) which was approximately 8 miles from Control Point, we also wore the same dusty and clothing (except for the coveralls) back to camp. When we though the clothes were dirty we put them in our laundry bag under our bed until we had a day to do our washing; They did not warn us of the danger we were in.

Our living quarters were nothing more than chicken coops. They reeked with sand and dust every, morning when we woke up. There were no windows, just pieces of plywood on the outside of the hut. We could go outside and open the 4'x 8' sheets of plywood, exposing the screen to let the wind blow through the hut. There was absolutely no glass in the building, we lived in these dusty conditions for three months after the first Atomic test, WHICH WAS ONLY EIGHT MILES FROM THESE SHOTS

Our outfit was the radiation safety group in 8 Atomic bomb detonations, as Armed Forces Special Weapons Group (AFSWP). Our RAD-SAFE training was very minimal, because they did not know any more than we did. The U.S. Government was more interested in perfecting the Atom Bomb before Russia did.

I know I was exposed to more radiation than the Government acknowledges on my film badge records. One reason is because, on at least two different occasions I transported to Colonels and a civilian scientist out to the side of a mountain on the test site. They chipped rocks and dug holes (retrieving test equipment). They stayed out so long, and because my Geiger counter was in the off scale area I had to threaten that I would have to leave them if they didn't immediately get in my vehicle so we could return to the Control Point. They insisted on staying longer to retrieve the equipment. I was very near saying goodbye to them.

96

I also worked in the vehicle decontamination area. We would run a vehicle upon a ramp like a grease rack, with the front end about four feet higher than the back end. Then we put in one package (2 to 3 pounds) of Tide soap into a barrel of water. We used this water to pressure wash the underside of the vehicle. While this process removed a lot of the radiation, it also got us soaking wet. We did this in our fatigues, which we wore back to the huts and put in our dirty clothes bag. This ramp was built on an uphill slope. The dirt and dust contaminated with radiation was rinsed off the vehicle and just ran down the slope until it dissipated. There was no way of cleaning up the radiation that just soaked into the ground the day or week before. This same ramp was used for all of the time we were at Camp Mercury without any possible way of getting rid of the radiation that had accumulated over the days or months prior to our use.

GENE TORONTO
US 55 038 062

As far as Nevada, my assignment was in supply, issuing out protective clothing to some of those going out into the contaminated area. I also checked it back in when the came back in from their assignment.

As far as I remember our living quarters were nine man huts about 20 to 30 miles from the Control Point. The shots were 10 to 20 miles from the Control Point, but I have no idea how far from our huts these shots were. I'm sure that many of the others had jobs that were more dangerous than mine.

You say Marines were hauled in. I always thought it was Army solders, and I heard they were only 1,000 yards from Point Zero. The vehicles were decontaminated on a rack just outside of the Control Point, where I worked.

There were about 21 shots and each one could have contaminated us.. but that is what you are trying to find out. Just how much? Although we were all there, some were exposed more than others because of what our jobs were.

GLENN WELLS
US 55 057 552

My experience at Camp Mercury was the usual radiation monitoring. I would take people out to the blast area after the test explosion. I did tiffs 8 or 10 times before I reached my maximum dosage. After this I was ordered to wash contaminated vehicles without a film badges or protective clothing. I did this 3 or 4 times before returning to Denver.

Another time under the command of a Navy Lieutenant, I was ordered to look for some stray cattle that had wandered into the Restricted Area. I remember we spent several hours driving all over the desert without film badges or protective clothing. We also had no Geiger counters. We never did find the missing cattle. I also believe the Navy Lieutenant had no idea if an area had radiation or not.

HERB HONG
US 55 038 023

I flew out of Nellis Air Base with several men on a cargo plane. From there, we went to Camp Mercury. I was assigned to a hut made out of plywood. For several days the wind would blow at the camp with a lot of dust being blown around. I was at camp with Dick True, James Hamilton, and other men who I am unable to remember.

I went out in the field one time with a Lieutenant one time. We checked the radiation reading , and it was high. There were a lot of Hot Spots in the field. We came in and changed our suits. We had our fatigues underneath these suits. We never changed our clothes and then we went back to camp without any radiation check being done. I can remember a lot of dust. I had film badges some of the time.

98

I have had a lot of health problems in my lifetime. I lost my right eye from cancer, and I also have prostate problems. In addition, I have bleeding ulcers and Sinus infection. I still think a lot of my trouble with my health is from atomic radiation.

I have a twin brother Herald. He has not had any health problems. He was never enrolled in the service

I feel now that we were used as Guinea Pigs. I have forgotten a lot of things we did after 44 years.

GERALD BACON
US 55 076 662

HISTORY OF THE ARMED FORCES SPECIAL WEAPONS PROJECT (AFSWP) RADIOLOGICAL SAFETY GROUP DURING OPERATION TUMBLER-SNAPPER (1952)

Operation TUMBLER-SNAPPER was an eight detonation atmospheric nuclear test series conducted at the Nevada Test Site from April 1,1952 to June 5, 1952.

During Operation TUMBLER-SNAPPER, the Atomic Energy Commission (AEC) established safety criteria to minimize the exposure of participants to ionizing radiation while allowing them to accomplish their scientific and military objectives.

Most radiologic safety procedures at the test site were performed by the Armed Forces Special Weapons Project (AFSWP) Radiological Safety Group. This organization was primarily composed of personnel from the 216th Chemical Service Company, an Army unit from Rocky Mountain Arsenal, Colorado. The AFSWP Radiological Safety Group also included personnel from the Navy and Air Force.

In general, the Radiological Safety Group was responsible for the following activities:

Training and preparing radiological monitor for their work and familiarizing participants with radiological safety procedures.

Issuing and developing film badges and evaluating gamma radiation exposures recorded on film badges.

Providing clothing, respirators, and other protective equipment.

Performing radiological surveys and controlling access to radiation areas.

Briefing observers and project personnel of radiological hazards and the radiological conditions in the test area.

Detecting and removing contamination from personnel and equipment.

The radiological Safety Group provided radiological safety monitors for all TUMBLER-SNAPPER shots. These monitors accompanied scientific and technical personnel on many project recovery missions in to the test area following nuclear tests. In addition, radiological safety personnel surveyed the shot area after each detonation and manned the checkpoints to radiation areas.

2 November 1989

Fact Sheet

Defense Nuclear Agency
Public Affairs Office
6801 Telegraph Road
Alexandria, Va. 22310-3398
(703) 325-7095
Facsimile Number (703) 325-2962

January 1994
Nuclear Test Personnel Review Program
Radiation Exposure in U.S. Atmospheric Nuclear Weapons Testing

Approximately 200,000 Department of Defense (DoD) military, civilian and contract personnel participated in U.S. nuclear tests that were Conducted during the atmospheric test series, primarily in Nevada and the Pacific Ocean. Many were exposed to low levels of ionizing radiation in the performance of various activities. The doses generally were within the current federal occupational radiation guidance (5 rem per year) and averaged about 0.6 rem. Approximately 1,700 personnel received doses in excess of the current federal occupational radiation guidance.

The Nuclear Test Personnel Review (NTPR) program, established by DoD in 1978 and administered by the Defense Nuclear Agency (DNA), provides test participants their recorded radiation exposure or assesses the most probable exposure. The basic means to measure dose from ionizing radiation at U.S. atmospheric nuclear tests was the film badge. Of the approximately 200,000 DoD participants in U.S. atmospheric nuclear tests, about 95,000 have film badge data available. The official repository for these records is maintained by the Reynolds Electrical and Engineering Company, a Department of Energy (formerly Atomic Energy Commission, AEC) contractor.

102

Individual dose information is available from DNA. Requests for such information may originate from individuals, representatives authorized under the Privacy Act, the Department of Veterans Affairs (VA), or Congress.

Until 1955 film badges were issued to some of the personnel in a. unit, such as a platoon, ship or aircraft. If everyone in the unit was expected to receive similar exposures only a few representatives might be badged. If some personnel were to perform functions not typical of the unit as a whole, then those personnel were individually badged. After 1955, DoD and AEC policy changed to require the badging of all participants. Some badges were environmentally damaged during their use and were rendered unreadable, and some records were lost or destroyed in the 1973 fire at the Federal Records Center in St. Louis. As a result, a significant portion of the NTPR effort has focused on assessing the exposure of personnel who were not issued film badges and those whose records are missing or incomplete.

DNA considers all relevant circumstances when performing radiation exposure assessments. Assessments begin with the determination of individual or unit activities and the relationship of such activities to the radiological environment.

If records indicate the location of personnel and it is clear that they were not exposed to a radiological environment, their dose is judged to be zero. In units where some members had film badges with valid readings and others did not have badges, doses for the unbadged personnel who participated in similar activities are inferred from the doses of their badged counterparts. Where there are insufficient badges, or where a common relationship to the radiological environment does not exist, dose reconstructions are performed.

Determination of No Dose Potential. DNA researches activities of an individual or his unit for the period of participation in an atmospheric nuclear test. Unit locations and movements are related to areas of radioactivity. If personnel were beyond the range of initial radiation (several miles) from nuclear detonations, did not experience fallout or enter a contaminated area, and did not come in contact with radioactive materials, they are judged to have received no radiation dose.

Dose Based on Film Badges of Others. DNA uses film badge data from badged personnel to derive individual doses for unbadged personnel. A group of participants is identified who had a common activity and thus a similar potential for exposure to radiation. Identification of these homogeneous groups is based upon research of historical records, technical reports, or correspondence. Using standard statistical methods, the film badge data are examined along with a description of personnel activities to determine their validity for use in the reconstruction and their assignment to the entire group. Often the dose or time distribution of badge readings indicates that the group should be subdivided into more similar groups before proceeding further with the analysis. For each homogeneous group, the mean dose, variance and confidence limits are determined, and the upper limit dose is then assigned to unbadged personnel. This ensures that personnel are assigned doses that are higher than the average for the group based on uncertainties in the activity description. If individuals cannot be associated with a specific homogeneous group, statistical derivation of dose is not used.

Dose Calculation. DNA performs rigorous dose calculations when film badge data are unavailable for any part (or all) of the exposure period. DNA also performs calculations if film badges are damaged and cannot yield reliable dose data, if unique activities are ascribed to specific individuals, or if neutron or internal radiation exposures to a target organ are indicated. These calculations involve correlating the activities of an individual or unit with a fully characterized radiological environment.

The calculation of dose is a standard scientific practice used by health physicists when the entire circumstances of radiation exposure require assessment. First, the conditions of exposure are reconstructed to include all known activities based on input from the individual as well as information from official reports and historical documents. The radiation environment is then

104

characterized in time and space, and collated with the activities and locations of the unit or the individual. In addition to gamma radiation that has been measured by film badges, the radiation environment includes neutron radiation for close-in personnel and beta and alpha radiation for personnel whose activities indicate the possibility of inhalation or ingestion of radioactive materials. Finally, the intensity of the radiation is determined for the entire period of exposure, from which the total integrated dose is calculated. An uncertainty analysis, which considers the values of all parameters used, provides a measure of the confidence of the calculations. Existing dosimetry is then analyzed and compared with the calculated dose to further enhance the confidence of the calculations. Where the potential existed for inhalation or ingestion of radionuclides, internal dose commitments to the target organ are derived and provided to the VA and/or to the individual. These are doses accrued over a 50-year period after exposure which, when added to the film badge or calculated whole body dose, represent the total dose to the target organ specified.

The above dose determination procedures have been reviewed by some of the country's leading scientists and were initially described in the *Federal Register* on May 20, 1982, and later amplified in the *Federal Register* on October 21, 1985. Subsequently, the National Academy of Sciences (NAS) completed a "Review of Methods Used to Assign Radiation Doses to Service Personnel at Nuclear Weapons Tests." The NAS Committee on Dose Assignment and Reconstruction for Service Personnel at Nuclear Weapons Tests found that:

> "...the procedures used to estimate external radiation doses were reasonably sound . . . .The NTPR has developed procedures that permit satisfactory estimates to be made of the external doses received by these participants. There are uncertainties in the dose estimates, but it appears that 99 percent of the personnel received doses of less than 5 rems, which is

approximately the average dose received by the general population during the last 30 years from exposure to natural radiation and the use of ionizing radiation during medical procedures Although the committee concentrated only on methods, it found no evidence that the NTPR teams had been remiss in carrying out their mandate. If any bias exists in the estimates, it is probably a tendency to overestimate the most likely dose, especially for internal emitters or when the statistical procedure for assigning dose is used ...."

DNA has developed the NTPR program to provide veterans with information relevant to their radiation exposure. Dose reconstruction, as noted above, is based on evaluation of available records. Test participants who can provide copies of personal records are invited to send them to DNA if it appears that their dose reconstruction is based on incomplete records. Further inquiries can be addressed to Defense Nuclear Agency, (ATTN: RAEM/NTPR), 6801 Telegraph Road, Alexandria, VA 22310-3398, or one may call 1-800-462-3683. In Virginia, call (collect) 703-285-5610.

The (NTPR) is making sure, that the very ones that deserve the wages, security and medical attention, that the veteran needed in his life for the last 50 years, will never receive it. The (NTPR) just keeps coming up with a figure, and although they know nothing about where you were or what you did in the tests, they will swear in court, if needed, that you are getting an accurate radiation dosage that regulates the kind of life this veteran, that served his country will receive, both physically and monitarily.

If they would have been in our shoes and done what we did, would these people that work for the (NTPR) accept the type of reconstruction they are giving us. You can bet they would be irate at the manner, that the reconstruction is being handled.

To me this is greed, to take away what a veteran really deserves, so that they themselves are able to live a happy and prosperous life, with security only for themselves. They really do not deserve their wages, healthcare and pension, that we earned serving our country. Did they serve their country for our healthcare? WE SERVED SO THE (NTPR) COULD CLAIM OURS.

The main problem is, they got by reconstructing our radiation dosages for 40 years before the "top secret files" were opened. and now that we know the truth we can't do anything about it.

Comments on Defense Nuclear Agency's Preceding Fact Sheet .
January 1994

In this fact sheet, published by the Defense Nuclear Agency dated January 1994, it states that there were approximately 200,000 Department of Defense personnel. They consisted of the Military, Civilian, and Contractors. I think this figure is intentionally low, because I have read in other Government printed material figures of 250,000 and 400,000. After 50 years and probably half of them dead, who can dispute the figures, when the U.S. Government is such a master at cover-ups and outright deceit?. This is one of the reasons we need a Congressional Investigation.

According to this Fact Sheet, "95,000 of these 200,000 have" (and listen to this) "FILM BADGE DATA AVAILABLE." What bothers me about this statement that is I think to make this or any other statement, the LT.S. Government should have to expose their records, and print how many of these *95,000* are confirmed Film Badge records and how many of the 95,000 personnel have a RECONSTRUCTED Dosage. I'm sure it would shock us all if we found out that our dosage was based on only 10,000 actual film badges, rather than the *95,000* figure. If we found out that the numbers which were put out 20 years ago of 400,000 personnel involved, this would mean that our dosage is based on <u>only five percent</u> of the actual film badges on record.

The point the Government is TRYING to make by making this statement is, they arc trying to install in your mind the 95,000 figure as a fact, hoping you will overlook the word "RECONSTRUCTED." Then you will have in your mind that what the Defense Nuclear Agency is saying is, that 50 percent of the test personnel have ACCURATE FILM BADGE RECORDS.

In fact, at the bottom of the page it says:

"Some badges were environmentally damaged during their use and were rendered unreadable, and some records were lost or destroyed in the 1973 fire at the Federal Records Center in St. Louis."

The following quote is more the truth than the rest of the page, if you read it carefully:

<u>"As a result, a significant portion of the Nuclear Test Personnel Review "NTPR" effort has focused on assessing the exposure of personnel who were not issued film badges and those whose records are missing or incomplete."</u>

Let's take a better look at the lower part of the page. The publication here again is trying to get you to believe that most of the people have been issued a film badge. Some facts will come up later in this book that arc records, and they will shock you. I would like to quote several sentences, and look very closely at what the couple of sentences actually say:

"Until 1955, film badges were issued to <u>some</u> of the personnel in a unit, such as a platoon, ship or air craft. If everyone in the unit was expected to receive similar exposures, only a few representatives <u>might</u> be badged."

The bottom paragraph (4) on the first page states:

"DNA considers all relevant circumstances when performing Radiation Exposure Assessments. Assessments begin with the determination of individual or unit activities and the relationship of such activities to the radiological environment."

I can't believe anyone sitting behind a computer, when I don't think they have any idea what went on out at the test site, can make any kind of a rational decision-then claim it to be accurate enough to stand up in court or base a veteran's physical condition, health, or compensation on. It would make about the same amount of sense to me to have a person given sworn testimony in court on what happened at an automobile collision in the next city, when he was not present, and knew absolutely nothing about an automobile, or how it operates.

After reading the 39 letters in this book written by the very ones who were the 197 AFSWP personnel, I cannot imagine taking anyone's word ahead of theirs. These 197 men in the Tumbler-Snapper Series of Atomic Band Tests had the hands-on experience of working daily with the radiation. They, AFSWP, were the ONLY PERSONNEL AT THE SITE WHO HAD ANYTHING TO DO WITH monitoring and mapping radiation around Ground Zero, fallout, filter stations, and aircraft cloud sampling within 340 km. of the test site. AFSWP, or these men, also were the only ones that were involved in the Personnel, Equipment and Vehicles Decontamination. If you have read what each one wrote, how could anyone possibly come to the conclusion that these men don't know what they are talking about, take some kind of theory, and disregard their word totally.

I will cite several cases in review of some of the things these men said in the letters and Questionnaires they mailed to me.

First of all in a letter from Paul A. Martin, he states that he and his partner were on the same shot, in the same vehicle (which broke down) at the same time, and Paul received 3.52 Roentgens of Radiation while his partner received 6.5 Roentgens. Both readings were Overdosed for the year on this <u>one shot and on one mission</u>. If the ones reconstructing Radiation dosages would have been at the scene at the time, <u>they would know how this could happen</u>. (I'll tell you like Paul did in his letter.) Paul stayed with the vehicle and did not get down on the ground. Instead he crawled out on the hood and made repairs to the vehicle, while the sergeant got scared and started to walk out. By the time Paul got the vehicle repaired, his partner had walked about two blocks when Paul drove up to him and picked him up. **SO THE QUESTION IS--HOW WOULD YOU RECONSTRUCT HIS PARTNER'S RADIATION DOSAGE IF HIS PARTNER DID NOT HAVE A FILM BADGE?** (Put yourself in our position with dosage reconstruction.)

A letter written to me in the book says, "I would sometimes have to work on some of the vehicles to make them ready to go out. So without a film badge at the HOT MOTOR POOL, I know I received unknown Radiation." (From letter from R. Duane Kraft)

"Thirty minutes after a surface shot, four of us were sent to the blast site as an initial survey team to get as close to Ground Zero as possible using Geiger counters." "We were in an area where the dust hadn't settled. Birds were fluttering, trying to fly but couldn't and were dying, and my badge changed complete color indicating over exposure. When we reported back to the Control Center (which if you recall was only seven miles from Ground Zero), the Officer in Charge chewed our asses out, because we got an overexposure and it would be inconvenient for him to send the required overdose report to Washington D.C." (From letter from Dick True)

On Page 3, Paragraph Number 1, I would like to quote from the Fact Sheet:

"In addition to Gamma Radiation that has been measured by film badges, the Radiation environment

110

includes neutron Radiation for close-in <u>personnel whose</u> <u>activities indicate the possibility of inhalation or</u> <u>ingestion of radioactive materials</u> (which are sand dirt, contaminated water, food or blowing dust)."

In the next statement in the same paragraph, it tells how the assessment for neutron, Alpha, and beta radiation, <u>which are</u> <u>particles that cannot be calculated by the Film Badge,</u> is determined for each Test Participant by the Defense Nuclear Agency (DNA) (which you will see is absolutely ridiculous).

"Finally, the intensity of the radiation is determined for the entire period of exposure, from which the total integrated dose is calculated."

Which is the total exposure on your Film Badges, or Film Badges <u>ASSESSMENTS</u>. A part of this Film Badge reading becomes your "ACCURATE" ingested Radiation Dosage. This determination does not, so far as I'm concerned, take into consideration the area in which you received your film badge reading.

The comparison I would like to make is this: one day you would be working on film badge records, the next on guard duty at an access gate checking for radiation on personnel and equipment, and some days issuing clothing.

In contrast to this, I was a Radiation Monitor, and according to a letter I mailed home on <u>April 25, 1952</u> (which I still have), it states I drove 250 to 300 miles every day. In between shots we would have to drive back and forth across the test site daily. One of my jobs was changing filters at stationary air filter stations in some of the cities within 340 km. of the test site, cities such as St. George, Utah, Ely, Nevada and the cities on the East side of Nevada.

The main reason we drove through the desert daily was to save time and mileage. It would save 150 to 200 miles one way by not going through Las Vegas. Driving through the test area across the dusty desert, ingesting the dust that was so heavy, a person could not see the vehicle if you were a quarter mile away from it. Control Point was always in a hurry to get the air filters to a plane at an abandoned or private air field, sometimes 80 or 100 miles from the filter stations. I might add that we <u>NEVER</u> had film badges when chasing the fallout or checking filter stations off site, even though we were driving across some of the earlier Ground Zeros to get to our destination. We also should have film badges when the filters were on the seat for 100 miles or sometimes more than two hours.

The whole point I am trying to make is to compare a person working in a Nuclear plant on a waxed floor with a person driving across a dusty desert with the windows open because we did not have air conditioning, ingesting Alpha and Beta particles into our lungs and stomach. If it were a simple as our government thinks it is to RECONSTRUCT radiation dosages, why not give the guard at the gate a film badge and just figure that anyone on the test site has the same amount of radiation as the guard?

The Nuclear Test Personnel Review (NTPR) program should be ABANDONED. It should never have been able to start in the first place. <u>The lawmakers shouldn't have been misled by the NTPR personnel who just wanted the wages and security at the expense of the veterans and the widows of those who have died in the service of their country</u>. **WHAT A DISGRACE**.

There are many other things that the Atomic Veteran has been denied. Whatever the veteran has was not from their service, or from radiation. It is possible to have psychiatric, mental, eye, ear, heart, lung. and I could go on and on for many pages about what any other veteran could have. If the Atomic Veteran doesn't have CANCER (a certain kind), then it is not from radiation .....

U.S. Department of Commerce
National Technical Information Service

ADA 122 242

OPERATION TUMBLER-SNAPPER 1952

JRB ASSOCIATES
MCLEAN, VA

JUN 82

Fact
Sheet

Defense Nuclear Agency
Public Affairs Office
6801 Telegraph Road
Alexandria, Va. 22310-3398
(703) 325-7095
Facsimile Number (703) 325-2962

Subject: Operation TUMBLER-SNAPPER

Operation TUMBLER-SNAPPER, a series of atmospheric nuclear weapons tests; was conducted by the Atomic Energy Commission (AEC) at the Nevada Proving Ground (NPG) from 1 April to 5 June 1952. The operation consisted of eight nuclear detonations in two phases. The TUMBLER phase, of primary concern to the Department of Defense (DOD), consisted of four weapons effects tests, Shots ABLE, BAKER, CHARLIE, and DOG. These airdropped devices were detonated to collect information on the effect of the height of burst on overpressure. Shots CHARLIE and DOG were also part of the SNAPPER phase, of primary concern to the AEC and the Los Alamos Scientific Laboratory. The other weapons development tests in the SNAPPER phase were Shots EASY, FOX, GEORGE, and HOW. The primary purpose of these four tower shots was to gather information on nuclear phenomena to improve the design of nuclear weapons.

Department of Defense Involvement

About 7,350 of the estimated 10,600 DOD participants in Operation TUMBLER-SNAPPER took part in Exercise Desert Rock IV. The remaining DOD personnel assisted in scientific experiments, air support activities, or administration and support activities at the NPG.

Exercise Desert Rock IV, an Army training program involving personnel from the armed services, included observer programs and tactical maneuvers. Observer programs, conducted at Shots CHARLIE, DOG, FOX, and GEORGE, generally involved briefings on the effects of nuclear weapons, observation of a nuclear detonation, and a subsequent tour of a display of military equipment exposed to the detonation. Tactical maneuvers, conducted after Shots CHARLIE, DOG, and GEORGE, were designed both to train troops and to test military tactics. Psychological tests were conducted at Shots CHARLIE, FOX, and GEORGE to determine the troops' reactions to witnessing a nuclear detonation.

Soldiers from various Sixth Army units provided support for the Exercise Desert Rock IV programs. They maintained and operated Camp Desert Rock, a Sixth Army installation located three kilometers south of the NPG. These soldiers provided essential services such as food, housing, transportation, communications, construction., and security. Some of the Desert Rock support troops worked in the forward areas of the NPG to construct observer trenches, lay communication lines, provide transportation, and assist with other preparations for Desert Rock IV activities. Many of the Camp Desert Rock support personnel observed at least one detonation during Operation TUMBLER-SNAPPER, and some were called upon to perform support or staff duties in the test areas during nuclear detonations.

115

DOD personnel also participated in scientific experiments conducted by two test groups at Operation TUMBLER-SNAPPER: the Military Effects Test Group and the Weapons Development Test Group. The Military Effects Test Group was sponsored by Test Command, Armed Forces Special Weapons Project (AFSWP), and involved more DOD participants than did the AEC Weapons Development Test Group. The Los Alamos Scientific Laboratory conducted most of the Weapons Development Test Group activities, but DOD personnel were sometimes involved. Test group participants placed instruments and equipment around ground zero in the days and weeks before the scheduled nuclear test. At shot-time, these personnel were generally positioned at designated observer locations or were working at substantial distances from ground zero. After each detonation, when it was determined that the area was radiologically safe for limited access, these participants returned to the test area to recover equipment and gather data.

DOD personnel also provided air support to Operation TUMBLER-SNAPPER. The Air Force Special Weapons Center (AFSWC), from Kirtland Air Force Base, had primary responsibility for cloud' sampling, courier missions, cloud tracking, aerial surveys of the terrain, and other air support as requested. AFSWC consisted of units of the 4925th Test Group and 4901st Support Wing, which staged out of Indian Springs Air Force Base.

Although the AEC Test Manager was responsible for planning, coordinating, and executing Operation TUMBLER-SNAPPER programs and activities, DOD personnel assisted in these duties. They were responsible for overseeing the DOD technical and military operations at the tests.

Summaries of TUMBLER-SNAPPER Nuclear Events

The eight TUMBLER-SNAPPER events are summarized in the accompanying table. The accompanying map shows the ground zeros of these shots.

Shot ABLE, an airdropped nuclear device, was detonated at 0900 hours on 1 April 1952, 793 feet over Area 5 of Frenchman Flat. ABLE had a yield of one kiloton. The event was a weapons effects test and involved DOD personnel from the Military Effects Test Group and the Weapons Development Test Group in about 30 scientific and diagnostic experiments. AFSWC activities included the airdrop, cloud sampling, courier service, cloud tracking, and aerial surveys. In addition, over 150 personnel from the Strategic Air Command observed the detonation from B-50 aircraft flying over the test area. No formal military training exercises were conducted at this shot, although 15 members of the Camp Desert Rock support staff witnessed the shot. Onsite radiation intensities were characterized by small areas of low-level radioactivity surrounding ground zero. Six hours after the shot, the 0.01 R/h* radiation intensity line was at a radius of about 600 meters from ground zero.

Shot BAKER, an airdropped nuclear device, was detonated at 0930 hours on 15 April 1952, 1,109 feet over Area 7 of Yucca Flat. The BAKER device had a yield of one kiloton. BAKER was also a weapons effects test and involved DOD personnel from the test groups in 45 experiments. AFSWC activities included the airdrop, cloud sampling, courier service, cloud tracking, and aerial surveys. About 170 Strategic Air Command observers flying in B-50 aircraft witnessed the detonation. No formal military training exercises were conducted, but ten members of the Camp Desert Rock staff did witness the shot. Onsite radioactivity was characterized by small areas of radiation around ground zero. About one hour after the shot, the initial radiological survey team found a radiation intensity of 1.2 R/h at ground zero, decreasing to 0.01R/h 750 meters south of ground zero.

Shot CHARLIE, an airdropped nuclear device, was detonated with a yield of 31 kilotons at 0930 hours on 22 April 1952 about 3,500 feet over Area 7 of Yucca Flat. About one hour after the shot, the initial survey showed that radiation intensities of 0.01R/h or more were confined within 1,000 meters of ground zero.

As part of Exercise Desert Rock IV, the armed services fielded a troop observer program with 535 participants and a tactical troop maneuver with about 1,675 participants. The tactical maneuver at Shot CHARLIE was conducted by the following units:

Army

- 2nd Battalion, 504th Airborne Infantry Regiment, 82nd Airborne Division, Fort Bragg, North Carolina

- Company B, 167th Infantry Regiment, 31st Infantry Division, Camp Atterbury, Indiana

- Company C, 135th Infantry Regiment, 47th Infantry Division, Fort Rucker, Alabama

*Roentgens per hour

- Tank Platoon, 11th Armored Cavalry Regiment, Camp Carson, Colorado

- Engineer Platoon, 369th Engineer Amphibious Support Regiment, Fort Worden, Washington

- Medical Detachment (augmented), Sixth Army, numerous Sixth Army posts.

Air Force

- 140th Fighter-Bomber Group (Provisional)
- 140th Fighter-Bomber Wing, Clovis Air Force Base, New Mexico

118

The CHARLIE tactical maneuver consisted of five activities:

- Observation of the shot
- Psychological testing
- Movement to objective
- Inspection of an equipment display
- Airborne exercise.

After observing the shot from trenches approximately 6,400 meters south of ground zero, the troops were tested by the Human Resources Research Office and the Operations Research Office to determine their reactions to the detonation. The troops then toured the display area and approached as close as 160 meters to ground zero, where they encountered radiation intensities of up to 0.01R/h. While ground troops were taking part in these activities, Army paratroopers landed in a drop zone north of ground zero. Some of the paratroopers, however, jumped prematurely and missed the drop zone by as much as 13 kilometers. Five paratroopers were slightly injured on landing. Despite this problem, the exercise was completed as planned.

In addition to Exercise Desert Rock activities, DOD personnel participated in about 50 scientific projects, approximately 190 Strategic Air Command observers witnessed the shot from aircraft flying in the vicinity of the NPG, and AFSWC personnel provided air support, including the bomb drop.

Shot DOG, another airdropped nuclear device, was detonated with a yield of 19 kilotons at 0830 hours on 1 May 1952. Ground zero for DOG, which was detonated more than 1,000 feet above Area 7, was the same as that for Shots BAKER and CHARLIE. The initial radiation survey, taken about one hour after the shot, showed that radiation intensities of 0.01R/h extended approximately 1,600 meters from ground zero.

119

The Navy and Marine Corps conducted a troop observer program and a tactical troop maneuver at Shot DOG as part of Exercise Desert Rock IV. The observer program involved approximately 350 Navy and Marine participants. Desert Rock participants observed the shot from trenches 6,400 meters south of ground zero. The tactical maneuver was conducted by about 1,950 Marines from the Marine Corps Provisional Atomic Exercise Unit. This unit consisted of officers and enlisted men from the 1st Provisional Marine Battalion of Camp Pendleton and the 2d Provisional Marine Battalion of Camp Lejeune. The DOG tactical maneuver was the first maneuver conducted by the Marine Corps during continental nuclear weapons testing. As at Shot CHARLIE, troops observed the shot, took psychological tests, and toured display areas. In addition, some participants accompanied AFSWP and Desert Rock monitoring teams on their initial survey of the ground zero area in Order to learn radiological monitoring techniques. At Shot DOG, three display areas were established between 270 and 1,600 meters from ground zero. The Marines stopped their tour of the displays at 820 meters from ground zero because of the radiation intensities they encountered.

In addition to Desert Rock activities, DOD personnel participated in about 50 of the scientific experiments conducted by the test groups, about 180 observers from the Strategic Air Command watched the detonation from aircraft flying in the vicinity of the NPG, and AFSWC personnel provided air support, including the bomb drop.

Shot EASY was detonated from a 300-foot tower at 0415 hours on 7 May 1952 in Area 1 of Yucca Flat. The device had a yield of 12 kilotons. DOD participants were involved in approximately 30 of the test group experiments, and AFSWC personnel provided air support. No formal Desert Rock IV training exercises were conducted. However, 1,000 personnel from Camp Desert Rock support units witnessed the shot from the Control Point at Yucca Pass. Onsite residual radioactivity was heaviest around and to the north of ground zero. The initial radiological survey team was unable to complete the survey on shot-day because of the large radiation area and rough terrain. On the day after the shot, the 0.01R/h line was 900 to 1,000 meters east, south, and west of ground zero but extended about six kilometers north of the shot-tower.

Shot FOX, a 300-foot tower detonation, was fired in Area 4 of Yucca Flat with a yield of 11 kilotons at 0400 hours on 25 May 1952. Most onsite fallout occurred to the northeast of ground zero, overlapping residual radiation from Shot EASY. Ninety minutes after the shot, the 0.01R/h line extended farther than 6.5 kilometers to the east. High radiation levels to the northeast prevented completion of the initial radiological survey on shot-day. Three days after the shot, the 1.0 R/h line extended less than 500 meters from ground zero, except to the northeast where it reached nearly two kilometers.

*6400 meters = 4 miles

During shot FOX, the largest single activity was the Army troop observer program, part of Exercise Desert Rock IV. Approximately 950 exercise troops from the 701st Armored Infantry Battalion, 1st Armored Division, Fort Hood, Texas, witnessed the shot from trenches 6,400 meters southeast of ground zero. An additional 500 observers from the six continental armies and the service schools also witnessed the shot. The observer program included psychological testing before and after the shot and a tour of the equipment display area.

In addition, DOD personnel were involved in 27 test group experiments. AFSWC personnel provided air support, and about 100 observers from the Strategic Air Command witnessed the shot from aircraft flying in the vicinity of the NPG.

Shot GEORGE, a 300-foot tower detonation, was fired with a yield of 15 kilotons at 0355 hours on 1 June 1952. GEORGE was detonated in Area 3. The initial radiation survey established the 0.01R/h line at about 1,300 meters to the west, south, and east of ground zero. The area north of the shot-tower could not be surveyed on shot-day because of radiation levels in excess of 10.0 R/h.

The Desert Rock troop observer program and tactical troop maneuver at Shot GEORGE involved approximately 1,800 Army troops. Immediately after they observed the shot from trenches about 6,400 meters south of ground zero, about 500 soldiers toured the equipment display area, located about 500 to 2,500 meters southwest of ground zero. The remaining 1,300 soldiers took part in the tactical troop maneuver, a ground assault on an objective south of ground zero. Immediately after the shot, the troops, accompanied by five tanks, advanced from the trench area toward the objective. When Army monitors preceding the assault detected radiation intensities of 0.5 R/h at about 460 meters from ground zero, the attack was halted. Troops then proceeded to the equipment display areas. The following Army units took part in this maneuver:

- 23rd Transportation Truck Company, Camp Roberts, California

- 31st Transportation Truck Company, Fort Ord, California

- Tank Platoon of the 1st Armored Division, Fort Hood, Texas

- 369th Engineer Amphibious Support Regiment, Fort Worden, Washington.

In addition to these Desert Rock activities, DOD personnel participated in 25 of the test group experiments, AFSWC personnel Performed air support missions, and 24 observers from the Strategic Air Command watched the detonation from two B-50s flying in the vicinity of the NPG.

Shot HOW was detonated from a 300-foot tower, located in Area 2 of Yucca Flat, on 5 June 1952 at 0355 hours. Shot HOW, the last weapons test of Operation TUMBLER-SNAPPER, had a yield of 14 kilotons. No Exercise Desert Rock programs were conducted, but DOD personnel did participate in about 30 of the test group projects. The onsite fallout pattern extended to the north and northwest of ground zero, but the initial radiological survey team did not monitor that area because no recovery operations were necessary there. The survey team did measure/intensities of 0.01R/h as far as two kilometers to the west of ground zero.

Safety Standards and Procedures

The Atomic Energy Commission established safety criteria to minimize the exposure of participants to ionizing radiation while allowing them to accomplish their missions. The AEC established a limit of 3.0 roentgens of gamma exposure per 13-week period for Exercise Desert Rock, the joint AEC-DOD organization, and most of AFSWC. AFSWC sampling pilots were authorized to receive up to 3.9 roentgens during the TUMBLER-SNAPPER operation because their mission required them to penetrate the clouds formed by the detonations.

The Test Manager was ultimately responsible for the safety of participants in Exercise Desert Rock IV, of the personnel in the joint AEC-DOD organization, and of individuals residing within 320 kilometers of the NPG. Most onsite and offsite radiological safety procedures were performed by the AFSWP Radiological Safety Group, composed of personnel from the Army, Navy, and Air Force. An officer appointed by Test Command, AFSWP, headed the group.

The Desert Rock Exercise Director was responsible for conducting Exercise Desert Rock IV in compliance with the AEC radiological safety policies. The Desert Rock Radiological Safety Group was usually supervised and assisted by the AFSWP Radiological Safety Group. The AFSWP group was also responsible for processing the 216th's AFSWP film badges worn by Desert Rock participants.

123

The 4925th Test Group (Atomic) implemented radiological safety procedures for AFSWC personnel at Indian Springs Air Force Base. For AFSWC personnel at Kirtland Air Force Base, the 4901st Support Wing (Atomic) carried out these procedures.

Although the missions and activities of each organization were different, the general radiological safety procedures followed by all groups were similar:

- Orientation and training - preparing radiologica monitors for their work and familiarizing participant with radiological safety procedures

- Personnel dosimetry - issuing and developing film badge and evaluating gamma radiation exposures recorded on film badges

- Use of protective equipment - providing clothing, respirators, and other protective equipment

- Monitoring - performing radiological surveys and controlling access to radiation areas

- Briefing - informing observers and project personnel of radiological hazards and the radiological conditions in the test area

- Decontamination - detecting and removing contamination from personnel and equipment.

Radiation Exposures at TUMBLER-SNAPPER

As of June 1982, the military services had identified by name 5,064 participants in TUMBLER-SNAPPER. Film badge data are available for 1,803 of these participants, as shown in the "Summary of Dosimetry for Operation TUMBLER-SNAPPER" table. Forty-two DOD participants who were subject to the joint

AEC-DOD participants who were subject to the joint AEC-DOD organization limit of 3.0 roentgens exceeded it, and eight individuals subject to the 3.9 roentgen AFSWC limit received exposures in excess of the stipulated level.

OPERATION TUMBLER-SNAPPER 1952
FROM
U.S. DEPARTMENT OF COMMENCE
NATIONAL TECHNICAL INFORMATION SERVICE
PUBLICATION JUNE 1982 REPORT #   6019F
GOVERNMENT ACCESSION NUMBER   ADA 122-242
SECURITY CLASS; UNCLASSIFIED

This is a technical report sponsored by the Defense Nuclear Agency. "This report describes the activities of an estimated 10,600 personnel, both Military and Civilian, in operation Tumbler-Snapper, the Third Nuclear Weapons Testing Series conducted at the Nevada Proving Ground."

The Tumbler-Snapper series of tests were pioneers in the atomic testing. To show what a threat, and how close the Russians were behind the United States, in Nuclear Technology, I will list the tests in order, up to and including 1953.

Series	Year	Location	Shots
1. Trinity	July 16, 1945	Alamogordo, New Mexico	1
2. Bomb	Aug.6, 1945	Hiroshima, Japan	1
3. Bomb	Aug.9, 1945	Nagasaki, Japan	1
4. Crossroads	1946	Pacific Ocean	2
5. Sandstone	1948	Pacific Ocean	3
6. 1st Atomic Test	Aug.9, 1949	Russia	?
7. Ranger	1951	Pacific Ocean	3

First Atomic Test at Nevada test site January 27, 1951

8. Greenhouse	Jan. 27, 1951	**Nevada test site**	4
9. Buster-Jangle	1951	Nevada test site	7

Total detonations by U.S. before Tumbler-Snapper 1952

24

10. Tumbler-Snapper	1952	Nevada test site	8

216th Tests are #25 # 26 # 27 # 28 # 29 # 30 # 31 # 32

1st Hydrogen Bomb detonated by U.S. Pacific	1953
1st Hydrogen Bomb detonated by Russia	Aug. 19,1953

Total Nuclear Tests at Nevada Test Site	926
Total Nuclear Tests by U.S. worldwide	1,051

The Fact Sheet tells the maximum radiation allowed, and also the jobs of AFSWP.

U.S. Department of Commerce
National Technical Information Service
Operation Tumbler-Snapper 1952
Report # 6019F Page #
Accession # ADA 122-242

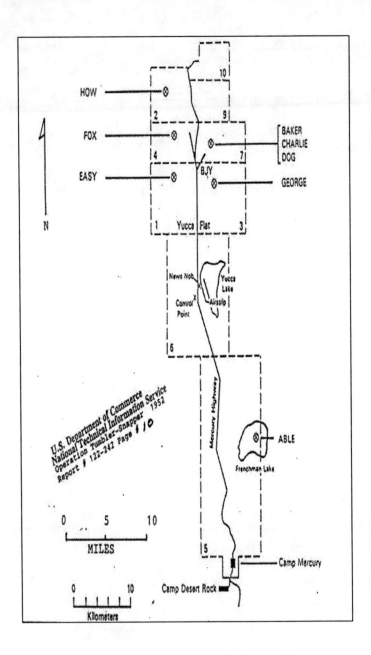

GROUND ZEROS FOR OPERATION TUMBLER-SNAPPER AT THE NEVADA PROVING GROUND

This is a map showing locations. Which is interesting in quite a few things that I think were not done properly. The first thing wrong was, The first shot "Able". It was detonated less than 10 miles from where we lived, in Camp Mercury, for the next 90 days. We also had to drive within 3 miles of that Ground Zero every day to get to work and back at our "Control Point". Why didn't the A.E.C. make this the final shot, just before we were ready to leave the area. We could carry Geiger Counters in Camp Mercury, but were not allowed to carry Film Badges. I'll quote one of the letters, in this book that was sent to me. "I was on a bus returning to Camp Mercury from the Command post through an area which should not have been "HOT". I mention this because at these times there were no film badges to measure an individual's exposure." We should have been able to have film badges at all times, especially Camp Mercury.

Service	Personnel Identified by Name	Personnel Identified by Name and by Film Badge	Gamma Exposure (Roentgens)					Number of Personnel with Zero Gamma Exposure*	Average Gamma Exposure (Roentgens)	Maximum Gamma Exposure (Roentgens)
			<.1	.1-1.0	1.0-2.0	2.0-5.0	5.0+			
Army	1786	843	285	463	61	17	7	215	.296	10.8
Navy	483	130	51	51	26	2	0	13	.594	4.2
Marine Corps	1880	25	22	2	1	0	0	21	.070	1.5
Air Force	416	416	177	184	36	17	2	88	.497	7.5
Scientific Personnel, Contractors, and Affiliates	389	389	208	98	72	12	1	118	.375	6.1
TOTAL	5064	1803	761	798	196	48	10	427	.468	

• The number of personnel in this column is also represented in the <.1 Gamma Exposure column.

I guess the first thing we have to consider is, this summary is dated June 1982. This is EXACTLY 30 years after our tests, which ended on June 5, 1952. The Defense Nuclear Agency would like you to believe that the figures of 5,064 Radiation dosages are accurate, but you are smarter than that. in the very next column the report states that there are only 1803 "identified by Film Badge."

What will scare you is the figures of the 216th. out of 10,600 personnel in the total test. If you look at the "ARMY", you will see that out of 843 only 24 were overdosed (over 3 Roentgens for the whole test). 12 of these 24 were members of the 216th Chemical Service Company, According to page 162 of the book "ADA 122 242 by U.S. Department Of Commerce, National Technical Information Service".

Of the total film badge look close at who got them. The Air Force, (who were running the program) out of 416 personnel there was 100% (416) received Film Badges. Then the 389

130

scientific personnel, Contractors, and Affiliates, got 100% (389) received film badges. FOR A TOTAL OF 815 FILM BADGES.

Out of these 2 groups was a total 815 personnel received 100% or they got 815 leaving only a total of 988 film badges for all of those in the test. So almost 50 % of the film badges were given to 2 groups, that were getting a 100% safety coverage.

In one group that had the most dangerous job in the tests. They monitored and mapped all radiation around Ground Zero on the ground and cloud tracking up to 340 km. of the test site. They did all of the decontamination of personnel, Vehicles, and Equipment. If there was a dangerous job the 216th had it. Yet only 74 out of 138, ever received one Film badge, so 64 or 45 % did not even get one film badge, even though they worked in the most contaminated areas every day. If you look at the figures out of 389 people that had 100 % film badge coverage, and only had 13 Overdosed. The 216th had only 74 film badges with 12 Overdosed.

There are many more facts here if you really look it over close.

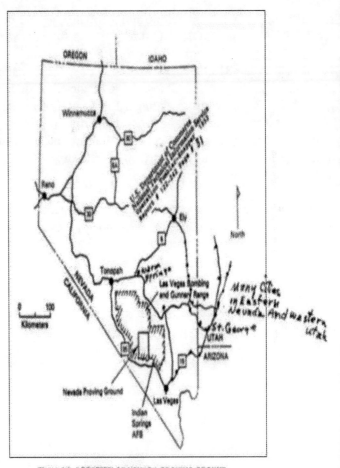

Figure 1-1: LOCATION OF NEVADA PROVING GROUND

When going off-site to Ely, or any place in Eastern Nevada, as well as Western Utah, down south as far as St. George, Utah, to locate the fallout or to change air filters in the filter stations, and meet planes at abandoned or private airfields, we were not allowed to carry Film Badges. Yet in order to save up to 150 miles, by not going South to Las Vegas. We were told to go across the test site. When we would go across the test site, and a lot of former Ground Zero's, we would be driving a quarter of a mile from the vehicle, you couldn't recognize it on account of the dust. We had no air conditioners, so the windows were always open, with a quarter of an inch of dust on our laps. **WE DID NOT REALIZE OR HADN'T BEEN TOLD ABOUT RADIATION THAT WE WERE INGESTING BY SWALLOWING OR BREATHING WAS BAD FOR OUR HEALTH**. As you have already read there was no way of measuring the alpha and beta radiation that we were ingesting, even if we would have had been issued Film Badges.

As long as we hadn't gone to the current detonation site, and or didn't have a film badge we didn't have to go through the Decontamination station. I personally never once took a shower at the Control Point Decon Station. I took my showers back at camp, and I have no idea where the radiation went.

The Radiological Safety Group established the radiological safety procedures used to limit the exposure of Desert Rock exercise troops entering the forward area. The Desert Rock Radiological Safety Group was independent of the AFSWP radiological safety group but conducted some activities under the direction of the AFSWP group with the assistance of the 216th Chemical Service Company which was attached to AFSWP. After each shot, Desert Rock radiological safety monitors accompanied troops into the forward area; conducted ground radiological surveys; monitored trenches, equipment displays, and troop maneuver areas; and decontaminated Desert Rock personnel leaving the forward area. Chapter 5 of this volume describes Desert Rock radiological safety activities in more detail (8; 14; 42; 91; 106; 109 160).

The Instructor Group conducted the orientation program for incoming troops and observers and briefed personnel on the objectives of Exercise Desert Rock IV, the capabilities of nuclear weapons, and the protective measures to take against the blast, thermal, and radiation effects of a nuclear detonation. The instructors were from the Sixth Army and AFSWP (8; 106; 108; 160).

The S-4 Section, Logistics, was responsible for providing logistical services to Camp Desert Rock and the exercise troops (106; 108; 160).

EXPLANATION OF "DESERT ROCK" RAD-SAFE UNIT

The Radiological Safety Group (RAD-SAFE) was independent of Armed Forces Special Weapons Project (AFSWP) "but conducted some activities under the direction of the AFSWP group with the assistance of the 216th Chemical Service Company which was attached to AFSWP."

The Desert Rock RAD-SAFE unit would go into the forward area or troop movement area, with their own troops, where on occasions, there were several thousand Desert Rock Military personnel on maneuvers. There were always a few AFSWP personnel to oversee the Desert Rock RAD-SAFE maneuvers. The Desert Rock RAD-SAFE UNIT monitored only their own personnel and the area or trenches that they were located in. The Desert Rock RAD-SAFE unit and their troops had almost NO Film Badges and very few Gieger Counters. (Radiation Detectors)

As long as we have been discussing "Desert Rock", which is a camp A little over a mile from Camp Mercury. It is just outside of the gate of Nevada Test Site. The next six pages is the information about the support group units, and the 7,350 troops in "Exercise Desert Rock IV". Where they were from, and what their jobs or duties were. According to the following page there was 7,350 troops in "Exercise Desert Rock IV". All of the support groups listed in these six pages also lived in Camp Desert Rock. I can't remember, but I am pretty sure this was a "TENT CITY". The total population for the entire State of Nevada was only 150,000.

This would leave a small amount of Civilian and military personnel stationed on the test sight or at Air Bases for Aerial Surveys and monitoring.

The next page said these Military personnel were allowed to "witness the Nuclear detonations from positions 6,400 meters from Ground Zero." Which is 3.8 miles. A news release, through records released, said that some Military personnel were positioned 1/3 of that distance, or at 1,024 yards which is 1.15 miles. According to uncovered Pentagon documents by Rep. Edward Markey D-Mass. (7-31-94 St.Paul Pioneer Press 11-A) I understand this shot was right after ours. (6 mos) It was shot Badger in 1953. As hard as the Nuclear Defense Agency tried to cover this up, leads me to believe that this sort of cover-up was an ongoing way of keeping the Military and public uninformed and quiet.

The U.S. Government is so good at this cover-up please read the sixth page after this. It is called Exercise Desert Rock IV ESTIMATED Number of Participants.

U.S. Department of Commerce
National Technical Information Service
Operation Tumbler-Snapper 1952
Report # 122-242 Page # 57

EXERCISE DESERT ROCK IV PROGRAMS AT OPERATION TUMBLER-SNAPPER

According to estimates compiled by the armed services, approximately 10,600 DOD civilian and military personnel took part in Operation TUMBLER-SNAPPER. Of these, an estimated 7,350 individuals participated in Exercise Desert Rock IV activities conducted by the Sixth Army.

Exercise Desert Rock IV was designed to train maneuver units in the effects of nuclear weapons. The objectives were to (108):

- Provide training in the tactical use of nuclear weapons

- Observe psychological responses to nuclear detonations

- Provide information on radiological safety measures

- Provide training in the effects of a nuclear detonation on ordnance materiel and military equipment.

While its objectives were similar to those of previous Desert Rock exercises, Desert Rock IV differed in certain respects.. For example, the AEC gave the Army greater responsibility for radiological safety. In addition, the AEC and DOD authorized troops to be positioned closer to ground zero to observe the shot and to conduct postshot activities; observers were allowed to witness the nuclear detonations from positions 6,400 meters from ground zero (71; 108; 120).

Department of Defense personnel involved in Exercise Desert Rock IV were assigned to Camp Desert Rock. DOD personnel at Camp Desert Rock were divided into two groups: Camp Desert Rock support troops and Desert Rock IV exercise troops (98, 108).

Camp Desert Rock Support Troops

Camp Desert Rock support troops numbered about 1,500 at Operation TUMBLER-SNAPPER. These troops were drawn primarily from the Sixth Army units listed below:

- Headquarters and Headquarters and Service Company,

- 369th Engineer Amphibious Support Regiment

- Shore Battalion, 369th Engineer Amphibious Support Regiment

  ■ Company D
  ■ Company E
  ■ Company F

- 562nd Transportation Staging Area Company (minus one platoon)

- 23rd Transportation Truck Company

- 31st Transportation Truck Company

- Company A, 505th Military Police Battalion

- Detachment, 314th Signal Construction Battalion

- Detachment, 504th Signal Base Maintenance Company

- Detachment, 3623rd Ordnance Medium Company

- Medical Detachment, Sixth Army

- 360th Army Band.

These units were generally stationed at the camp throughout the test series. They provided support services to the exercise troops, as described in chapter 2 (2-7; 98; 108).

In addition to their duties at Camp Desert Rock, some support units entered the forward testing areas of Yucca Flat and Frenchman Flat to help prepare for specific Desert Rock activities, assist in operations during test events, and help ensure safe recovery operations following a nuclear detonation. The Desert Rock Radiological Safety Group and the Instructor Group were two of these elements. The tasks of the Radiological Safety Group are discussed generally in chapter 2 and specifically in chapter 5 of this volume.

The Instructor Group prepared and conducted orientation programs for Observers and maneuver troops. Before shot-day, this group presented a basic orientation course on nuclear weapons effects, personal protection, and shot-day procedures. During the rehearsal of shot-day exercises, instructors took personnel on tours of the equipment display areas. On shot-day, participants arrived at the trenches about 90 minutes before the detonation. Instructors then began their orientation over the loudspeakers. After the shot, the instructors led maneuver troops and observers through the display area and discussed the effects of the detonation (101; 102; 108).

Other support personnel entering the forward area were from the following units:

- Camp Desert Rock Signal Detachment
- Medical Detachment, Sixth Army
- 23rd Transportation Truck Company

- ■ 31st Transportation Truck Company
- ■ Company A, 505th Military Police Battalion
- ■ Shore Battalion, 369th Engineer Amphibious Support Regiment.

These units usually entered the forward area only when large numbers of exercise troops were present, as at Shots CHARLIE, DOG, FOX, and GEORGE (101-103; 108).

The Camp Desert Rock Signal Detachment installed radio and wire communications systems, including a public address system, in each main trench area. On shot-day, participants operated two mobile public address systems consisting of trucks with loudspeakers. After the shot, they moved the system into the display area, where the Instructor Group used the loudspeakers to make presentations (101-103; 108).

Medical personnel present at Camp Desert Rock for Operation TUMBLER-SNAPPER were from the Sixth Army. Operations orders specified that, during the events, a medical detachment would move to the forward area and establish an aid station in a parking area. In addition to these medical personnel, the Camp Desert Rock Surgeon was in the forward area on shot-day and remained at the forward command post throughout the exercise. The units that participated in the maneuvers sometimes provided their own medical support (101-103; 108).

The 23rd Transportation Truck Company and the 31st Transportation Truck Company transported exercise troops from Camp Desert Rock to the trench area. They then moved the vehicles to a parking area farther to the rear. After the detonation and postshot activities, the vehicles were returned to the troop loading areas to transport the exercise troops back to Camp Desert Rock (101; 102; 108).

Company A, 505th Military Police Battalion, controlled the movement of Exercise Desert Rock vehicles in the forward area. Some of the military police were posted at entrances to the shot area, while others accompanied the units moving from Camp Desert Rock to the trench area. After the exercise troops had been taken to the trench location, the military police went to the parking area. After the detonation, they returned to posts at the road junctions to direct traffic from the trench area along the return route to Camp Desert Rock (101; 102; 108).

Another support element participating in the forward area was the 369th Engineer Amphibious Support Regiment, Members of this regiment customarily entered the forward area before a shot to construct trenches and equipment displays and after a shot to inspect and retrieve display items. Regiment personnel also participated as maneuver troops at Shot GEORGE (101; 102; 108).

Desert Rock IV Exercise Troops

About 7,350 Department of Defense personnel participated in TUMBLER-SNAPPER as Desert Rock IV exercise troops. These exercise troops represented each of the-armed services.

Unlike the support troops, the exercise troops were stationed at Camp Desert Rock for short periods ranging from several days to about two weeks (108).

Exercise Desert Rock IV consisted of two programs'

■ Troop observation and indoctrination to acquaint military and civilian DOD personnel with the effects of nuclear detonations
■ Tactical troop maneuvers to train participants in the use of nuclear weapons and to demonstrate the effects of nuclear detonations.

Table 3-1 indicates the estimated number of DOD participants in each activity at each shot.

The remainder of this chapter summarizes the Desert Rock IV programs as they were conducted during Operation TUMBLER-SNAPPER. Detailed descriptions of specific projects performed at each test of the series are presented in the TUMBLER-SNAPPER multi-shot volumes.

3.1 TROOP OBSERVER PROGRAM AT EXERCISE DESERT ROCK IV

The purpose of the observer program was to familiarize members of the armed services with the characteristic effects of nuclear detonations. Participants witnessed a nuclear event in the forward area of the Nevada Proving Ground and toured a display of ordnance materiel and military equipment arrayed in the vicinity of ground zero before and after the nuclear detonation.

Table 3-1: EXERCISE DESERT ROCK IV, ESTIMATED NUMBER OF PARTICIPANTS AT OPERATION TUMBLER-SNAPPER, BY PROGRAM

Program	Participating Service	ABLE	BAKER	CHARLIE	DOG	EASY	FOX	GEORGE	HOW
Observers	Army	0	0	300	0	0	950	500	0
	Army (Camp Desert Rock)	15	10	*	*	1,000	*	*	0
	Navy	0	0	0	300†	0	0	0	0
	USMC	0	0	0	50†	0	0	0	0
	Air Force	0	0	235	0	0	0	0	0
	Unknown	0	0	0	0	0	500**	0	0
Tactical Troop Maneuvers	Army	0	0	1,300	0	0	0	0	0
	Army (Camp Desert Rock)	0	0	*	0	0	0	1,300	0
	USMC	0	0	0	1,950	0	0	0	0
	Air Force	0	0	375	0	0	0	0	0
	Navy	0	0	0	0	0	0	0	0

* Unknown

* Unknown

† A combined total of 350 Marine Corps and Navy personnel has been documented; the breakdown by individual service is an estimate.

** These observers were from the continental armies and service schools.

The word estimated really bothers me, such as the title of this page. It says, "ESTIMATED NUMBER OF PARTICIPANTS." It is really a wonder that they admitted to ESTIMATING instead of the FACTS.

It is printed all the way through this book that there were a total of 10,600 people involved in the test. This doesn't look like what they have written throughout it. If they want to mislead us, they should have gone a little further and said, We had 10,600 Observers, and a few people in the test. THE main thing I would like to point out is the ERRORS. If you look involved in the test, BUT ARE OBSERVERS. If you would look at the very next two pages in this book, you will see the personnel marching into trenches only a couple of miles from Ground Zero....They are called Observers, ever though it says in this book that they were on maneuvers, given psychological tests, and other duties to perform. Where is the truth ? ?

If they can't reconstruct EVEN how many people were there, the branch of service they were in, or who they were, how in this world can they reconstruct their Film Badge Dosage. "ACCURATE"

Why does the Department of Nuclear Energy even allow this kind of documentation in their books ? In the first place if they have to estimate, they really don't know the answer, but they will try to make you believe they do know, In my opinion they sit down and say, We have to print something, so lets guess. If I were to guess and try to convince someone that what I'm saying is the truth, I would not use "ROUND NUMBERS".

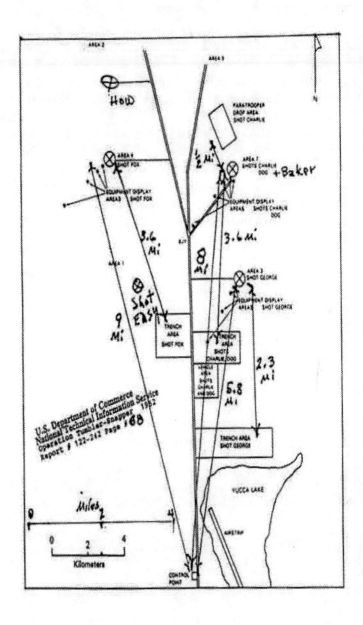

144

Figure 3-1: EXERCISE DESERT ROCK IV TRENCH AND DISPLAY AREAS, NEVADA PROVING GROUND, OPERATION TUMBLER-SNAPPER

This map may not be any more accurate than the most of this book, but I'll draw the mileages as platted.

1 km.= .62 mile

Control Point to Charlie, & Dog . . . . = 8 miles

Control Point to Fox . . . . = 9 miles

Control Point to George . . . . =5.8 miles

Shots they forgot to put on the map. Able, Baker, Easy & How.

There is no other map of these missing shots in this book.

(What good is the map) I guess it's a good space filler.

Fox Trench area to shot Fox . . . . 3.6 Mi.

George trench area to shot George . . . . 2.3 Mi.

Charlie trench area to shot Charlie . . . . 3.6 Mi.

Dog trench area to shot Dog . . . . .3.6 Mi.

Paratroopers jumped within 1/2 mile of the largest Atomic Bomb ever detonated in the world. Up until that date. (31 Kilotons)

It was more than twice as powerful as the Bomb dropped on Hiroshima, Japan, that killed 80,000. People. It was shot Charlie

Figure 3-2: OBSERVERS FILING INTO TRENCHES BEFORE THE
DETONATION OF SHOT CHARLIE, 22 APRIL 1952

All of the way through this book I've read about
"PROTECTIVE CLOTHING", Which we did not have except
for a pair of ordinary coveralls, once in a while. By the looks of
these personnel, it doesn't look like they had any protective
clothing either. In fact these men didn't even have the coveralls.
In the first eight men there are five different types of hats. Some
of these men had Fatigues, dress clothing, and everyday
clothing. One thing the same about all of them is, they have open
shirt collars. By the way these men were within 4 miles of
Ground Zero, in these trenches.

On page # 147 of the book U.S. DEPARTMENT OF
COMMERCE REPORT # 122-242 I will quote the protective
clothing as it is listed.

146

"Proper wear of protective clothing included closing openings in the coveralls with masking tape. protective clothing included: coveralls" (ordinary type) fatigue suits and caps shoes and boots white cotton gloves Rubber chemical gloves "end of quote in all of the time I was at the test site I never did see a single pair of rubber gloves or a Gas Mask. I must have been in the wrong place, but several times I was at Ground Zero.

None of the above had coveralls for a shot twice the size of Hiroshima, Japan.

Figure 3-3: MANEUVER TROOPS LEAVING FOXHOLES AND TRENCHES
AND BEGINNING THE ADVANCE TOWARD THEIR OBJECTIVE

This picture should convince you about the protective clothing. These men are charging Ground Zero. They have no gas masks, no coveralls, (called protective clothing), no cloth booties, because you can see the heels of their boots.

According to report # ADA 122-240 (DNA 6019F) page # 53 the men walked 4 miles to within 1/2 mile of Ground Zero. This must have taken 3 to 4 hours. Right after the shot Fox. also in the same book on page # 87 the troops again walked to within 1/2 mile of Ground Zero. it took approximately 4 hours. This was shot George.

148

If this area near the march was 1. Roentgen Per hour. these men were overdosed for the year. There was only 25 film badges in the 1950 men and you can bet the top brass had them. you could make another bet that the ones that had the film badges didn't walk 4 miles in and 4 miles out, especially with a full field pack..One roentgen is almost no radiation. display area under the direction of the Desert Rock Instructor Group. They then boarded trucks and returned to Camp Desert Rock (101-103; 108).

Associated with the troop maneuvers at TUMBLER-SNAPPER was a study of the psychological reactions of troops participating in the maneuvers. The Human Resources Research Office (HumRRO), a civilian agency under contract to the Department of the Army, and the Operations Research Office (ORO) performed the study at Shots CHARLIE, FOX, and GEORGE. A similar study had been performed during Desert Rock I at Operation BUSTER-JANGLE in 1951. The agencies were particularly interested in observing troop behavior in the trench area immediately before and after the detonation and measuring the changes in troop attitudes about nuclear weapons before and after participation in the indoctrination exercises and the Desert Rock maneuvers. The data collected by HumRRO and 0RO assisted the Army in determining the expected performances of troops involved in nuclear warfare. This page doesn't need a lot of explanation. We could use some explanation on the outcome of these Psychological tests if the Atomic Energy Commission would level with us.

Then again if the facts of these psychological tests were as distorted as the radiation dosage results are, we really wouldn't need the results at all.

I guess the results turned out negative for the Atomic Veteran. The rest of the military can have psychological problems, BUT NOT THE ATOMIC VETERAN. Again the only thing we can get is cancer. If the U.S. GOVERNMENT wanted to do a study, they should have done it on an "AFSWP" Organization. they are the ones that were in the most Radiation.

SUMMARY OF OPERATION TUMBLER-SNAPPER EVENTS (1952)

Shot	ABLE	BAKER	CHARLIE	DOG	EASY	FOX	GEORGE	HOW	Hiroshima Japan	Nagasaki Japan
Sponsor	DOD-LASL	DOD-LASL	DOD-LASL	DOD-LASL	LASL	LASL	LASL	LASL		
Planned Date	1 April	15 April	22 April	29 April	6 May	13 May	20 May	27 May	Aug. 6	Aug. 9
Actual Date	1 April	15 April	22 April	1 May	7 May	25 May	1 June	5 June	1945	1945
Time*	0900	0930	0930	0830	0415	0400	0355	0355		
NPG Location	Frenchman Lake (Area 5)	Area 7	Area 3	Area 7	Area 1	Area 4	Area 3	Area 1		
Type of Detonation	Airdrop	Airdrop	Airdrop	Airdrop	Tower	Tower	Tower	Tower	Air drop	Air drop
Height of Burst (Feet)	793	1,109	3,447	1,040	300	300	300	300		
Yield (Kilotons) ####	1	1	31	19	12	11	15	14	15	21

* Pacific Standard Time

1 Kilotons is the equivalent of 1,000 tons of T.N.T. (explosive power). Above is a comparison chart of each bomb.

The scheduled date is listed for each bomb. This could vary a day or two on account of adverse weather. That is until you come to Shot Fox. This Shot threw all of the rest of the test off schedule by being almost two weeks late (12 Days).

In the report # 6021F on page 48 it states that "Shot FOX was originally scheduled for 13 May 1952 but was rescheduled for 25 May because of a misfiring of the device and adverse weather conditions." To me it was a DUD. It took two men several days walking across the desert, pulling wires out of the ground, trying to find out why it didn't detonate when it was supposed to. Control Point thought it was a broken wire until the two men got to the tower, and then they thought it might be a relay stuck. They climbed the 30 story (300 ft.) tower, only to find that some one forgot to connect the wires to the detonator. This whole test was like a "Laurel and Hardy Comedy".

It tells the time of the Shot, Airdrop or Tower Shot, location on the test site, the height of detonation above ground, the explosive power of each bomb, And also a comparison of the two bombs detonated in Japan, that ended WW 11.

If you compare the power of the test bombs with the power of the bombs dropped on Japan, you will notice that Shot Charlie was more than twice the size of the bomb dropped on Hiroshima, Japan that killed between 80,000 and 140,000 people. These tests we had were not toys.

U.S. Department of Commerce
National Technical Information Service
Operation Tumbler-Snapper 1952
Report # 6019P Page # 30
Accession # ADA 122-242

Spheres approximately 1,000 to 1,740 meters from ground zero. After the declaration of recovery hour, they spent about one hour retrieving the spheres (57; 134).

Project 4.5, Flash Blindness, was conducted at Shots CHARLIE and DOG by the Air Force School of Aviation Medicine. Participating in the Project were personnel from the Air Training Command, SAC, and the Brooke Army Medical Center. The objective was to determine to what degree the flash of a nuclear detonation impairs the night vision of personnel. The protection afforded by the use of high-density goggles was also evaluated.

The test subjects witnessed the detonation from a darkened trailer about 16 kilometers from the point of detonation, near the Control Point. Twelve portholes along the side of the trailer were fitted with shutters to expose the eyes of the subjects to the nuclear flash. During the exposure, half wore protective goggles, while the other half did not. Following the exposure, the subjects were required to read lighted instruments to determine how soon they could perform visual tasks (54; 591 134; 157).

Project 4.6, Time Course of Thermal Radiation as Measured by Burns in Pigs, was conducted at Shots CHARLIE and DOG by the Naval Medical Research Institute and the University of

151

Rochester Atomic Energy Project. The Naval Medical Research Institute provided test equipment, while the Atomic Energy Project supplied the animals and conducted the biological experiments. The project was designed to study the production of skin burns in pigs.

On the day before each detonation, project personnel weighed the pigs and inspected their skins. From six to three hours before the detonation, personnel transported the pigs to display area under the direction of the Desert Rock Instructor Group. They then boarded trucks and returned to Camp Desert Rock (101-103; 108).

Associated with the troop maneuvers at TUMBLER-SNAPPER was a study of the psychological reactions of troops participating in the maneuvers. The Human Resources Research Office (HumRRO),a civilian agency under contract to the Department of the Army, and the Operations Research Office (ORO) performed the study at Shots CHARLIE, FOX, and GEORGE. A similar study had been performed during-Desert Rock I at Operation BUSTER-JANGLE in 1951. The agencies were particularly interested in observing troop behavior in the trench area immediately before and after the detonation and measuring the changes in troop attitudes about nuclear weapons before and after participation in the indoctrination exercises and the Desert Rock maneuvers. The data collected by HumRRO and ORO assisted the Army in determining the expected performances of troops involved in nuclear warfare (44; 61;101-103; 108; 110; 162).

ONE OF THE GUINEA PIG TESTS

PAGE # 92 of report # ADA 122-242

I always try to say that I was under the Atomic Bomb To gain the technology to keep ahead of Russia, in the development of the Atomic Bomb before they developed it. Russia hated the United States, and they had intentions of taking over the United States.

In a recently released article of 10/12/94.

"In Feb. 1953" (about 8 months after Tumbler-Snapper tests ended) "After eight years of experiments without a consistent set of rules to govern them, Charles E. Wilson, then Secretary of Defense, prepared a memorandum saying that "volunteers should be used as the only feasible means for realistic evaluation and/or development of effective preventive measures of defense against atomic biological or chemical agents" the memorandum added, "the voluntary consent of the human subject is absolutely essential."

The memorandum recommended using the Nuremberg Code which if actually applied, would be stricter than current practices because it required detailed explanations of the hazards of experiments regardless of any claimed benefits, and allowed the subjects to terminate experiments at any moment. But the present guidelines (1953) remained so highly classified that few if any people below the Secretaries of the Army, Navy or Air Force were aware of them.

Staff members of the advisory committee said this created the zen-like question, "what is the effect of adopting ethical guidelines which are then kept top secret?"

By 1951 it was clear to the Military and their medical establishment that it would be necessary to answer in detail many questions about the affects of radiation on humans, and that soldiers would have to be used as guinea pigs.

In September 1951 (6 moths before our tests) the joint panel on the medical aspects of Atomic Warfare prepared a memorandum saying that there were numerous reasons to conduct human experiments in atomic bomb explosions, and later documents show that at least four of the human experiments mentioned were carried out.

Among the problems that required experiments on humans, the panel said, were whether atomic explosion caused changes in visual acuity or light blindness, (THIS IS PAGE # 92) whether radiation from the explosions could be measured in the body fluids of people near such blasts, whether any psychological damage might come from being near an atomic explosion and whether flight crews would have any important exposure if they flew near a nuclear blast, each of the experiments was carried out.

In other experiments, airplanes flew through radioactive clouds. A report on one such test, begins, "The objective of this project was to measure the radiation dose, both from neutrons and gamma rays, received by an air crew delivering an MB-1 rocket." crewmen swallowed radiation film to help measure their exposure in operation "Plumb Bob."

This one test on PAGE 92 was designed to see how well the soldiers could perform after exposure to the flash of atomic detonations at night. "Human Volunteers were dark-adapted in a light tight trailer approximately 10 miles from Ground Zero. Their eyes were exposed to the flash. Some eyes were protected by a red filter, and some were unprotected."

The notes on the experiment said, "The project was terminated after shot 4 in order to evaluate the significance of lesions of the retina which were produced in two of the subjects."

In another experiment from this book ADA 122-242 "troops were brought to within 5,000 yards of Ground Zero to watch atomic explosions, and Several thousand were marched to the site of the detonation Just after the bomb had gone off." (WITH

ALMOST NO FILM BADGES) It is not yet known' what
happened to the subjects of these and other experiments.

Radiological safety activities within 320 kilometers of the
Nevada Proving Ground. The Atomic Energy Commission and
Test Command, AFSWP, established radiological safety criteria
for positioning personnel at nuclear detonations (91).

5.1 RADIATION PROTECTION FOR EXERCISE DESERT ROCK IV

The AEC was responsible for the overall operation of the
NPG, including the radiological safety of all Desert Rock IV
participants. Through AFSWP, the AEC established criteria to
protect Exercise Desert Rock IV participants from the thermal,
blast, and radiation effects of the TUMBLER-SNAPPER nuclear
tests. A 24 March 1952'letter from Headquarters, Test
Command, AFSWP, addressed the physical and radiological
safety of Desert Rock participants. The letter established a
maximum radiation exposure limit of 3.0 roentgens for Desert
Rock IV troops during the exercise. The AEC set a requirement
that maneuver troops and troop observers be at least 6,400
meters from ground zero during Operation TUMBLER-
SNAPPER detonations (25; 58; 108; 134).

5.1.1 Orientation and Briefing
The Exercise Desert Rock IV Instructor Group conducted
four orientation sessions for observers and exercise and support

troops, covering basic characteristics and effects of nuclear weapons, as well as personal protection procedures and related medical issues. In addition, the Instructor Group accompanied participating troops and observers on a tour of the shot area a few days before the detonation.

The orientation sessions had several deficiencies. To begin with, the instructors were not organized soon enough to prepare their teaching materials. The instructors who conducted the first two courses were not thoroughly familiar with nuclear weapons effects. Experienced AFSWP instructors were not available until the third orientation session, from 12 to 24 May. Finally, the Camp Desert Rock training aids were inadequate (42; 108). 6 of the 8 shots were completed by the 25th of May.

5.1.2 Personnel Dosimetry

Desert Rock personnel entering the forward area during Operation TUMBLER-SNAPPER were to wear film badges to measure their exposure to ionizing radiation. The Signal Section obtained film badges from the AFSWP Radiological Safety Group and issued them to participants no later than 1800 hours on the day before the shot. After the troops had completed their activities and returned to Camp Desert Rock, Signal Section personnel collected the film badges by 1800 hours on shot-day. The Signal Officer then returned the badges to the AFSWP Radiological Safety Group, which processed and interpreted them to determine individual exposure to radiation (91; 108).

5.1.3 Protective Equipment

According to the operations orders and the Desert Rock Final Report of Operations, Desert Rock troops entering the forward area on shot-days carried protective masks, which were worn on command. Figure 5-1 shows Marines rehearsing use of protective masks before the maneuver at Shot DOG. Although Desert Rock troops wore no special protective clothing, they were required to keep their standard fatigues tucked securely into their boot tops and to keep their sleeves and collars tightly buttoned to minimize contamination of underclothing and skin (102; 103; 108).

5.1.4 Monitoring

Radiological ground surveys of the test area generally began after the shock wave passed and when the Test Director gave

It is unbelievable that the Atomic Energy Commission (AEC) would tell the truth, about anything. So to admit that no one knew anything about what we were there for is a disgrace, when in most cases they have distorted the facts to cover up their blunders and mistakes. We had too many blunders and mistakes, in the Tumbler-Snapper series that overshadowed our accomplishments, and sometimes we were not to proud of the Director of Operations, and the Radiation Safety Director. It all boils down to the facts of: If the teacher doesn't know any of the answers, how can he teach us anything ??

I will only quote what the records say

On pages 128-9 of book # ADA 122-242 paragraph 5.1.1

"Orientation and Briefing"

I think we should look at each one of these remarks individually.

1. "The orientation sessions had several deficiencies."

If the AEC knew the orientation sessions had several deficiencies, then what was the point of even having the sessions? They should have remedied the deficiencies, or not had the sessions at all. I can not believe the AEC gave us these orientation sessions, and had the Gall to let us think of these instructors as our Idols. These were supposed to be the people that were going to keep us from harm, and tell us if there any dangers in radiation, and what the dangers were.

157

2. "the instructors were not organized soon enough to prepare their teaching materials."

This is the way the whole test was run. In other words they didn't have time to teach us, and they were unconcerned about our health or what happened to us physically or mentally. When we came to a problem, we were supposed to deal with it on the spot. We were expected to know what and how to treat every situation, and protect ourselves from harm. The only sad thing about the whole scenario is, they kept telling us "everything was O.K." and "don't worry it won't hurt you." When actually they didn't know if they were even in trouble themselves.

3. "The instructors who conducted the first two courses were not thoroughly familiar with Nuclear Weapons affects."

If these instructors were not familiar with the effects of nuclear weapons, I do not hold this against the instructors. It is the fault of the Test or Radiation Safety Directors, again. The instructors were ordered to teach, just like we were ordered to do a job we knew absolutely nothing about. Was it just the fact that the Test Director did not have time to be concerned about the things he considered INSIGNIFICANT. I think with his attitude of what was and was not important, and what he caused his troops to do and later on suffer from, is ABUSE OF POWER, AND ABSOLUTELY UNFORGIVABLE. He should have to stand trial for dereliction of duty, mental problems, or War Crimes against humanity. To have absolutely no concern for the safety of the personnel he was in charge of is in the least, INSANE.

4. "Experienced AFSWP Instructors were not available until the third orientation session from 12-24 May."

This is like locking the doors after the horse has been stolen. If experienced instructors were not available until May 24th, it did not help any of the troops learn about the affects of the Radiation that they were wallowing in during the first six of the eight shots total, in our series. By this date we had already completed six shots, and the damage had been done. The instructors that didn't know what they were teaching us had already convinced us that radiation was just a word, and we could lay down and sleep in it, and it wouldn't hurt us. We only had two of the eight shots left, and we had done such a good job and no one was dead yet. So if we wanted to we could complete the last two smaller shots, "standing on our heads." I really can not understand, after being 3/4 done with the whole tests, why they even instructed us at all. It was more of a waist of time than anything.

5. "FINALLY, THE CAMP DESERT ROCK TRAINING AIDS WERE INADEQUATE."

The last phrase the AEC used in this paragraph, speaks for itself. This paragraph, and especially this last phrase, is probably the only truth in the whole book. If only our Government would FINALLY ADMIT the same thing publicly, it would help the Atomic Veteran. Instead they hide the truth in one small paragraph in the middle of one book.. They will probably read it and before they admit to the truth, they will say, this is a misprint.

On another paragraph on this _same_ page I will quote.

The AEC has said all of the way through that we had protective clothing in the forward area. It says in paragraph 5.1.3 on "Protective Equipment"

"Desert Rock troops entering the forward area on shot days carried protective masks, which were worn on command." "Although the Desert Rock troops wore no special protective clothing, they were required to keep their standard fatigues tucked securely into their boot tops and keep their sleeves and collars tightly buttoned to minimize contamination of under clothing and skin."

Here the AEC admits that we never got any protective clothing. In some places the book -swears we all were protected, (with coveralls) and another place it says we didn't get anything. Also, in all of the time I was in Nevada I personally never seen a protective mask, and you would think of all people, the 216th Chemical Service Company would have protective masks.

These pages tell the responsibilities, activities, expectations and personnel make-up of (AFSWP).

The Armed Forces Special Weapons Group (AFSWP) organized and appointed the Radiological Safety Group (RAD-SAFE) which was supposed to address the issue of Radiation Safety of everybody within 250 miles of the Nevada Test Site, which later changed it's name to Nevada Proving Grounds. This was an uphill struggle because all we were told was that we should not have more than 3.0 Roentgens (r) of radiation. The Atomic Energy Commission (AEC) told us when we were monitors for the Air Force, for cloud sampling we were allowed 3.9 roentgens of radiation, we never did figure out why some of us were allowed 3.0 (r) and others 33 % more than what our allowable limit was supposed to be. The AEC kept telling us we didn't have to know any answers, all we had to know what our orders were, and follow them. The AEC said they would take care of the technical things. I wish they knew 40 years later what

they had done to the personnel that had trusted them on page #
133 is a graph, that is known as the Chain-Of-Command in the
tests. If you notice the "Top Brass" is the Test Director and the
Radiation Safety Director. Then everyone else under those two
are the Military personnel known as (AFSWP). On this same
page it spells out specifically, the different jobs we had to do
with 197 men.

On the next page # 134 it lists the following personnel and
where they are from. I guess the reason I keep going back to
show who AFSWP is and what they did is to prove that the men
that wrote the 39 letters were in the hottest spot in the tests.
These men didn't Just give some second hand story. They were
there. The records prove that they were there and also what they
were ordered to do.

Also on page ~ 134 of this report # 6019F it says. "The
following elements made up the AFSWP Radiological Safety
Group."

PERSONNEL   ORGANIZATION

UNIT..ENLISTED..OFFICERS.

138	134	4	216th Chemical Service Company
15	14	1	995th Quartermaster Laundry Company
9	7	2	17th Chemical Intelligence Detachment
10	5	5	Department Of The Navy
10	0	10	Department Of The Air Force
10	7	3	Test Command AFSWP
5	0	5	Headquarters, AFSWP
---	---	---	
197	167	30	

Vehicles and equipment were also first brushed in the forward area to remove dust. If this measure failed to reduce the radiation intensities to 0.01R/h or lower, vehicles were driven onto a rock bed at the decontamination station and washed with detergent and water. After each washing, monitors measured the contamination level with portable survey instruments. If repeated washings would not reduce contamination to permissible levels, the vehicles were isolated and allowed to stand until radioactive decay reduced contamination levels to 0.01R/h or lower. When radiation levels had been reduced below that limit, the vehicles were returned to service at Camp Desert Rock (102; 103; 108).

5.2 RADIATION PROTECTION FOR THE JOINT AEC-DOD ORGANIZATION

The Test Director was responsible for the radiological safety of all members of the Joint AEC-DOD organization at the Nevada Proving Ground during Operation TUMBLER-SNAPPER. The gamma exposure limit established for TUMBLER-SNAPPER participants was 3.0 roentgens, with the exception of the cloud-sampling pilots and crew who were permitted to receive exposures up to 3.9 roentgens.* To ensure that both onsite and offsite radiological safety procedures were followed, the Department of Defense established the Radiological Safety Group (25; 134).

The Radiological Safety Group was organized as shown in figure 5-2. Appointed by AFSWP, the Radiation Safety Director implemented the Test Director's radiation protection policy, which addressed the radiological safety of all persons within 320 kilometers of the Nevada Proving Ground. To implement this policy, the Radiation Safety Director supervised and

*The radiological safety report indicates that 3.9 roentgens was the established limit at TUMBLER-SNAPPER (91). However, this limit, except for the sampling crews, has not been verified in any other pre- or post-action report.

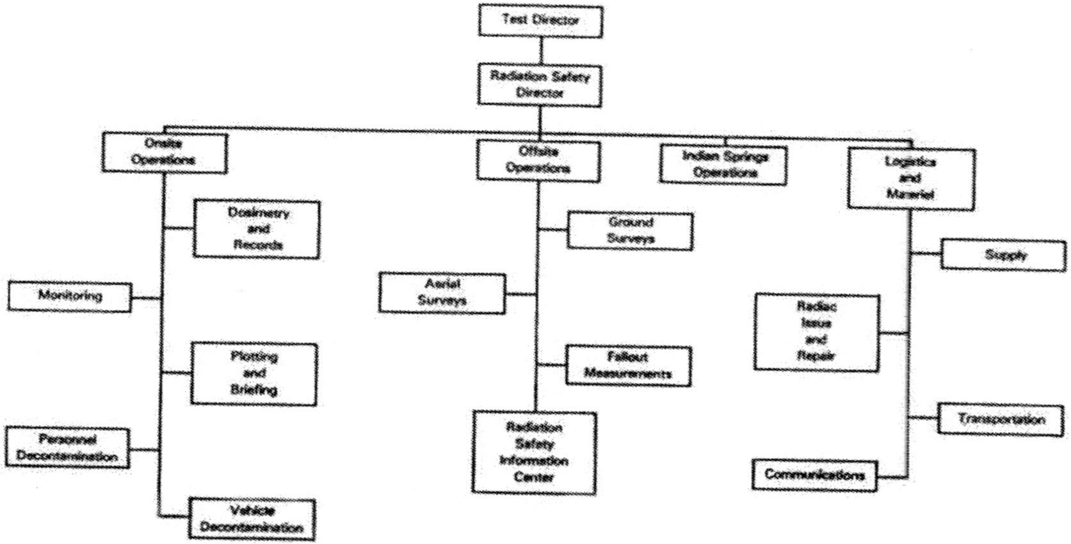

Figure 5.2: AFSWP RADIOLOGICAL SAFETY ORGANIZATION

Test Director
Radiation Safety Director
Offsite Operations
Indian Springs Operations
Logistics and Materiel
Onsite Operations

Ground Surveys
Fallout Measurements
Aerial Surveys
Radiation Safety Information Center

Supply
Transportation
Communications
Radiac Issue and Repair

Dosimetry and Records
Plotting and Briefing
Vehicle Decontamination
Monitoring
Personnel Decontamination

On the bottom of page # 134 and the top of page # 135 it lists the specific activities of 197 men called AFSWP.

Page # 135, it lists their "Operations", and page # 136 is the "Dosimetry and Records." In this section all of our problems of the atomic tests are originally generated. If you do not understand this book or the cover-up in it, that's O.K., but please understand this one page and the orders that were handed down to our officers in charge.

First of all, the known facts of our company was that the Test Manager or Director, Colonel Bussey, ordered 50,000 film badges at the beginning of The Tumbler-Snapper series of tests. He was censured by Washington, D.C., for this "ridiculous" order, and almost transferred out. Because the A.E.C. considered the need of a film badge to be "of no great importance in these tests."

If we used today's standards in a nuclear power plant, the test would have used the 50,000 film badges in less than five days. We had 10,600 personnel in this test series. If each one was issued at least one badge a day, for five days, we would have used **53,000** film badges in just five of the 91 days we were there. In the whole 91 days of the project, we only used a total of 1,803 film badges. To go a step further, if each one of the 10,600 personnel was issued only one film badge, for one day, we would have been 8,797 badges short, for just the one day. So when you look at what really happened, Our **dosage was reconstructed from less than 1/10th of 1 % of the total personnel that were involved in the tests.**

If you realize that some of the Scientists, Pilots and Monitors that had to go in to retrieve or read their experiments and map the Isointensity lines every day around Ground Zero. I am sure that some of these men got 2 or 3 film badges for each of the eight bombs. This would mean that one person might have as many as 18 film badges throughout the complete test series. So, if 100 individuals each had 18 film badges, This would total 1,800 film badges, and that is all we used on the whole test.

164

Ask yourself how accurate can your reconstructed dosage be, if 10,600 personnel is based on only 100 people that were only issued film badges once in a while.

We have seen documented in the records, and added into this book, the fact that two groups on this test were issued a film badge for each person. This was the Air Force, scientific personnel and contractors, and for each one of these two groups that were recognized by name were issued at least one film badge each, during the tumbler-Snapper series of tests. According to page # 161 of report # 6019F, accession # ADA 122-242. then again, only 5,064 were recognized by name out of the 10,600 that were present for the test.

Also, you have to realize that by June of 1982 when this report was published, over half of the 5,064 were probably names that were reconstructed, because the A.E.C. really didn't care to keep track of who was there.

It is really hard to pin down who needed a film badge, and didn't get one, especially if you don't even know what their names were, and what the individual's location in the test was. When you think of 1,950 Marines on one shot alone, got out of their trenches, with no protective clothing or masks, and spent several hours marching with a full field pack to GROUND ZERO and back to the parking area. According to the report these Marines only had 25 badges. I'm sure a lot of these 25 badges were in a Jeep and not walking in the dust and radiation. Some of the other ones that had to go without a film badge were the offsite monitors that were mapping the fallout and working at the off-site air filtering stations. The decontamination crews, motor pool, dosimetry and records people that were handling the contaminated film badges, "Hot motor pool" mechanics, dispatcher, the instrument callibrators and I could go on and on until I list the whole 10,600.

If you were issued one of the film badges you were not allowed to wear it back to Camp Mercury, which was inside the gates of the test site. There were two more gates to get to the Control Point from Camp Mercury. You would have to drive

165

within two to three miles of "ABLE" Ground Zero going from the camp to the Control Point and back every day. Our contaminated dirty laundry bag was under our bunks until wash day . I'm sure if we would have had the film badges issued to us we would have been overdosed many times more than the limit.

The reason we did not have film badges is because they were not issued. On page # 136 Of report # 6019F it states very clearly. "The onsite Operations Officer determined daily requirements for film badges and pocket Dosimeters for the groups taking part in the test." The Test Manager was holding our lives in his hands. This next statement is especially bad if you are not sent into Ground Zero. But after you are dispatched to three or four other places and then finally wind up at Ground Zero, without a film badge. This is also on the same page (136). "A film badge and dosimeter will be provided to official reentry parties and other personnel entering controlled radiation area. This is an area with radiation inten-sities exceeding 0.01 r/h." This means you don't get a badge if you have a job chasing fallout, decontamination or a hundred other things.

If you notice in another report # 6021F on page # 78 you will see that for the duration of Shot Fox, or one week, only 340 film badges were issued, this was from the 25th of May through the 1st of June.

The real disgrace is, on Shot Fox on page # 65 of report 6019F the graph shows that there were 1300 (estimated) troops on maneuvers, with orders to charge Ground Zero after the detonation and another 500 observers in the trenches.

With only 340 film badges issued this whole shot, how can they send 1800 men in to Ground Zero. Some on maneuvers and some inspecting the equipment displays, that were right next to Ground Zero.

If one person received a film badge every day like the nuclear plants of today, there would have been enough for 49 men. So 340 wouldn't even take care of the scientists and contractors. This is leaving nothing for the monitors or pilots.

This test was no different than any of the other Shots. I just used Shot Fox as an example. According to the records there were only 1,803 film badges issued in the duration of the whole test. If you divide eight shots into 1,803 you will find out that there should have been 225 film badges issued per shot. So actually 340 film badges was more than our share for Shot Fox. It makes you wonder, which one of the other shots was 115 film badges short.

PLEASE tell me how anyone can use these facts and figures and come up with a reconstructed radiation dosage, at least accurate enough to base another persons life or healthcare and compensation on.

Please look over page 139. It says the Isointensity lines were updated frequently , and at least daily around Ground Zero and the fall out areas, so the monitors should have had extra film badges, because they went back many time for new readings.

On page 140 it is a misrepresentation of the facts, we could not, or should I say it is not possible to measure alpha and beta particles with the instruments that were issued to us. The next error is, we did not have any steam. We had only soap and water to decontaminate the vehicles and equipment.

Another error is, it says we had a building, and we absolutely did not have a building to decontaminate the vehicles in. The only building in the whole area was the Control Point (or office) and a semi trailer about 50 feet away from the wash rack for storage of soap for decontamination of the vehicles and equipment. I washed my vehicle on the wash rack many times when I came in late out of the desert.

One other paragraph on page 142 I'd like to clear up. It says, that the vehicles in the hot park could not be removed without the approval of the vehicle decontamination Officer. I talked to some of the decon team, and they said there was no such thing as a Decon Officer. And I personally never seen one.

Coordinated all activities of the Radiological Safety Group and informed the Test Director of onsite and offsite radiological conditions. The Radiation Safety Director was also responsible for radiological safety operations at Indian Springs AFB (91; 134).

The following elements made up the AFSWP Radiological Safety Group (53; 91):

138 216th Chemical Service Company, consisting of four officers and 134 enlisted men from Rocky Mountain Arsenal, Colorado

15 995th Quartermaster Laundry Company Detachment, involving one officer and 14 enlisted men from Fort Devens, Massachusetts

9 17th Chemical Technical Intelligence Detachment, consisting of two officers and seven enlisted men from the Army Chemical Center, Maryland

10 Five officers and five enlisted men from the Department of the Navy

10 Ten officers from the Department of the Air Force

10 Three officers and seven enlisted men from Test Command, AFSWP

5 Five officers from Headquarters, AFSWP.
----
197 Total

The activities performed by the AFSWP Radiological Safety Group included (91):

• Advising the Test Director on measures to ensure the radiological safety of all personnel involved in the operation

• Furnishing all ground monitoring services for both scientific programs and radiological safety procedures within a 320-kilometer radius of the NPG

•Providing current radiological situation charts and maps showing onsite and offsite data obtained by ground and aerial surveys of the terrain

• Issuing, processing, and maintaining records of all personnel dosimeters

• Operating decontamination facilities for personnel vehicles, and equipment

• Receiving reports from cloud-tracking aircraft to advise the Test Director of the need to close air lanes

• Packaging radioactive material for shipment offsite.

5.2.1 Onsite Operations

The Onsite Operations Department was organized into five sections (91):

·   Dosimetry and Records
·   Monitoring
·   Plotting and Briefing
·   Personnel Decontamination
·   Vehicle Decontamination.

Members of these sections were responsible for all onsite radio-logical safety activities. Specifically, they were to (91; 134)'

- Provide test participants with film badges and pocket dosimeters

- Provide radiation monitors for test group projects

- Conduct initial radiation surveys and delineate radiation areas in the field by marking the 0.01, 0.1, 1.0, and 10.0 R/h isointensity lines

- Maintain onsite radiation intensity maps

- Brief recovery personnel on radiological conditions in the shot area before recovery operations

- Control access into radiation areas

- Monitor and decontaminate personnel, vehicles, and equipment returning from radiation areas

- Process film badges and maintain film badge exposure records.

Dosimetry and Records

For Shots ABLE, BAKER, CHARLIE, and DOG, the onsite unit of the Logistics and Materiel Department supervised the Dosimetry and Records Section. On 3 May 1952, the Dosimetry and Records Section was transferred from the Logistics and Materiel Department to the Onsite Operations Department (91).

The Dosimetry and Records Section was to provide a DuPont Type 558 film badge and one or more self-reading pocket dosimeters to official reentry parties and other personnel entering a controlled radiation area (an area with radiation intensities exceeding 0.01 R/h). Section personnel processed film badges for all test participants, including Desert Rock personnel (91; 134).

The Onsite Operations Officer determined daily requirements for film badges and pocket dosimeters for the groups taking part in the tests. A dosimetry clerk recorded the name, rank, service number (if appropriate), organization, and project affiliation of each participant in the group. He entered the data onto Form R1O1, the Daily Record of Radiation Exposure. This form, filled out in duplicate, listed the film badge number by the name of each individual using the device.

The dosimetry clerk issued the duplicate copy of Form R1O1, together with the film badges and pocket dosimeters, to the monitor accompanying the party, or to the party leader if a monitor was not required. The Dosimetry and Records Section retained the original copy of Form R1O1 pending return of the dosimeters. Upon completion of the mission, the monitor or party leader collected the dosimeters and returned them and the copy of Form R1O1 to the clerk at the Dosimetry and Records Section.

Film badges were sent along with Form R1O1 to the film badge processing laboratory in the Radiological Safety Building at the Control Point. The film badges were processed by 0800 hours on the following day. After developing the badges, members of the Dosimetry Section determined the net optical density, or darkness, of the film. Using a standard calibration curve, they then determined the radiation exposure indicated by various film densities. Dosimetry personnel entered the density reading and the exposure reading on Form R101.

In addition to Form R1O1, the Dosimetry and Records Section maintained Form R102, Individual Accumulated Radiation Exposure Record, as a permanent record of cumulative individual exposure. At the completion of the daily dosimeter processing, members of the Dosimetry and Records Section transferred information from Form R101 to Form R102. They sent cumulative exposure records for each individual to the Radiological Safety Director. The names of individuals who had accumulated more than 2.0 roentgens of gamma radiation exposure were underscored (91; 134). At the end of Operation TUMBLER-SNAPPER, the Dosimetry and Records Section compiled the records of individual total exposures into a report (22; 91).

Monitoring

The Monitoring Section performed the daily monitoring assignments required by the Ohsite Operations Officer. assignments included (91; 134):

- Conducting initial ground surveys of shot areas

- Posting signs warning of radiation areas

- Operating checkpoints

- Accompanying program and project personnel into areas with radiation intensities greater than O. 1 R/h.

Monitors conducted initial ground surveys soon after each detonation, beginning from several minutes to almost an hour after shot-time. The initial survey party, probably four or five two-man teams, traveled in radio-equipped vehicles to the shot area where they took radiation intensity readings. Beginning with Shot BAKER, these readings were taken along stake lines already laid out at the eight major compass headings from ground zero. Monitoring teams moved inward along the stake lines toward ground zero, taking radiation intensity readings at 90-meter intervals until they reached an intensity of 10.0 R/h. The monitors radioed information on the radiation intensity, location, and time to personnel in the Plotting and Briefing Section, who then drew radiation isointensity contour maps. The monitoring teams usually resurveyed the shot area on several

172

days after the detonation. Occasional variations of these procedures are indicated in the discussions of monitoring within the TUMBLER-SNAPPER multi-shot volumes.

The sign-posting detail, consisting of one officer and four enlisted men, posted signs and placed road barricades in radiation areas as directed by the Onsite Operations Officer. Members of the detail placed signs daily on barricades delineating the 0.01R/h lines on all main and secondary access roads. This detail was also responsible for positioning signs on the 0.1R/h isointensity line.

Checkpoint monitors were responsible for ensuring that each party entering a controlled area had a properly authorized area access clearance form issued by the Onsite Operations Office. The checkpoint monitors made sure that the names and numbers of individuals in the party and its protective equipment agreed with the entries on the form. If the form was filled in correctly, the monitor entered the time of entry on the document and returned it to the party proceeding into the forward area. When the party returned to the checkpoint, the monitor filled in the exit time and submitted the form on that day to the Onsite Operations Office, where the documents were filed (33; 91).

In addition to processing area access forms, the checkpoint monitors surveyed personnel and their equipment with Beckman MX-5 survey meters and provided the party with brooms to sweep dust from themselves and the equipment. The primary purpose of this preliminary decontamination was to prevent contaminated dust from accumulating on personnel (91; 134).

Plotting and Briefing

The duties of the Plotting and Briefing Section included plotting radiological situation maps based upon information provided by survey parties. Members of this section, who worked in the Plotting and Briefing Room of the Radiological Safety Building, developed maps showing the location of 0.01, 0.1, 1.0, and 10.0 R/h isointensity areas. They updated these

173

maps daily, or as often as resurveys were conducted. The Radiological Safety Director received up-to-date copies of these maps.

A member of this section briefed the leader and monitor of each party before that party entered a controlled radiation area. The briefing included an explanation of the radiological conditions in the area, of the location of checkpoints, and of the radiological safety regulations for radiation areas. After completing his presentation, the individual who had given the briefing signed the area access clearance form for the party and gave the form to the party monitor or leader (91; 134).

Personnel Decontamination

The Personnel Decontamination Section was responsible for monitoring and, if necessary, decontaminating individuals returning from radiation areas. One monitor, positioned outside the entrance to the Personnel Decontamination Section, directed all individuals to remove tape, booties, and gloves, in that order, and to put them in designated receptacles. All gloves and booties were considered contaminated without monitoring. Next, two monitors with Beckman MX-5 portable survey instruments surveyed personnel in the checkroom, as shown in figure 5-3. Outer garments and equipment registering radiation levels in excess of 0.007 R/h of gamma radiation, or undergarments and external respirator surfaces registering levels in excess of 0.002 R/h of beta and gamma radiation, measured about five centimeters from surfaces, were turned in to a member of the Supply Section. After this check, personnel took showers. One monitor was stationed at the shower exit to check skin contamination. Personnel showing radiation intensities in excess of 0.002 R/h returned to the showers (91; 134).

Vehicle Decontamination

The Vehicle Decontamination Section was responsible for monitoring and decontaminating equipment and vehicles returning from contaminated areas. Vehicles and equipment leaving the test area were stopped and monitored for contamination at checkpoints. Vehicles and equipment registering less than 1,000 counts per minute of alpha contamination per 55 square centimeters, less than 0.002 R/h of gamma radiation outside, and less than 0.002 R/h of gamma plus beta radiation inside passed through the checkpoints. Vehicles and equipment exceeding these radiation levels were sent to the decontamination station (91; 134).

Decontamination consisted initially of washing the contaminated item with steam and hot soapy water on a ramp and allowing it to drain. Personnel monitored the vehicle or equipment after it was washed to determine whether the decontamination was successful. If the radiation intensities had not been reduced to less than 0.002 R/h, the washing and monitoring procedure was repeated until the contamination was reduced to the desired level If contamination could not be reduced after five or six washings, the vehicle or equipment was placed in a "hot park" adjacent to the decontamination building until radioactive decay (No Building in 1952) reduced contamination building until radioactive decay reduced contamination to an acceptable level. The hot park was supervised by decontamination personnel, and vehicles or

Figure 5-3: MONITORS SURVEY PERSONNEL RETURNING FROM THE FORWARD AREA

The above picture must have slipped by the A.E.C., to be printed here. The picture looks innocent enough. That is until you <u>happen</u> to notice the sign on the wall in the background. This sign is a perfect example of the poor judgment or complete disrespect for our health and lives of the test director and the

Radiation Safety Director. **we didn't know, except what we were told.**

I'll bet they had their personal film badges every day, and all of the records to back the readings up, while they are sitting in their office.

THE SIGN ABOVE.

First of all, you are not allowed to check out, what they call protective clothing, unless you are going into the forward or radiation area. Then the sign says, plain as day.

YOU ARE ALLOWED TO KEEP YOUR CONTAMINATED CLOTHES AND WEAR THEM FOR 5 DAYS.

ONE OTHER THING, THE PROTECTIVE CLOTHING CONSISTS ONLY OF a PAIR OF COVERALLS AND COTTON CLOTH BOOTIES. These booties are like a pair of socks, over your boots, and the coveralls are no better than your fatigues equipment could not be removed without approval of the Vehicle Decontamination Section Officer. Personnel periodically monitored vehicles and equipment in the hot park, and when the radiation intensities had decayed to less than 0.002 R/h, the vehicles and equipment were returned to service (91; 134).

5.2.2 Offsite Operations

The Offsite Operations Department consisted of about ten officers and 50 enlisted men. Under the command of the Offsite Operations Officer, this department was responsible for radiological safety within 320 kilometers of the Nevada Proving Ground. The main function of the Offsite Operations Department was collating reports from aerial radiological surveys and offsite ground surveys in order to prepare maps showing offsite radiological conditions. Personnel assigned to this department also measured the airborne and surface concentration of radioactivity in various areas and determined the offsite fallout pattern (91; 134).

The department consisted of the following subsections:

- Ground Surveys

- Aerial Surveys

- Fallout Measurements

- Radiation Safety Information Center.

Monitoring teams in vehicles conducted ground surveys up to 100 kilometers from the NPG. The two-man mobile teams, who were in radio contact with the Radiation Safety Information Center, varied in number at the shots from eight to 13.

Aerial surveys consisted of cloud tracking and terrain surveys, both of which are discussed in chapter 4 of this volume. B-25 and B-29 aircraft tracked the cloud resulting from the detonation at various altitudes by flying as close to the cloud as possible without exceeding radiation intensities of 0.002 to 0.005 R/h. Monitors in C-47 and L-20 aircraft conducted aerial surveys of the terrain at heights of 500 to 1,000 feet. These surveys were used to delineate the offsite fallout pattern.

Other offsite personnel operated air-sampling and fallout stations. Approximately 18 of these stations, located from 30 to 320 kilometers from the NPG, were operated for at least 24 hours after each detonation.

Finally, one officer and six non-commissioned officers operated the Radiation Safety Information Center at the Control Point. Information from ground and aerial surveys was radioed to the center, where plots were made showing the fallout path and the radiation levels at offsite locations (91; 134).

5.2.3 Logistics and Materiel

The Logistics and Materiel Department furnished the Radiological Safety Group with supplies, equipment, transportation, and communications. This department consisted of the following sections (91; 134):

· Supply
· Rediac Issue and Repair
· Transportation
· Communications.

The Supply Section issued supplies, including protective equipment, on a daily basis.

Personnel in the Rediac Issue and Repair Section issued instruments for detecting beta and gamma radiation. They repaired and calibrated these instruments as needed after use. Personnel in this section were also participants in Project 6.1, Evaluation of Military Radiac Equipmen.t (91; 151).,

The Transportation Section operated a 24-hour motor pool, with at least one mechanic on duty at all times. Members of this section, which maintained military vehicles only, kept a daily record of all vehicles dispatched and returned.

The Communications Section operated and maintained the equipment used to radio survey results from the field to the Control Point (91; 134).

5.2.4 Indian Springs Operations

Although this department followed the standard procedures established by the Radiological Safety Group, it operated independently because of the special mission of AFSWC. Details of AFSWC's radiological safety operations are presented in the next section (82; 91; 134).

5.3 RADIATION PROTECTION FOR AIR FORCE SPECIAL WEAPONS CENTER PERSONNEL Including 1 Man from AFSWP.

During Operation TUMBLER-SNAPPER, the Air Force Special Weapons Center provided two types of air support to the test groups: test air operations and support air operations. The test air operations included all aircraft directly involved in test missions and projects, such as cloud sampling and cloud tracking. Support air operations included all other aircraft not directly involved in these test missions, such as sample couriers.

The radiological safety of air and ground personnel involved in AFSWC test and support operations vas the responsibility of the Test Director. He adopted the Joint AEC-DOD organization's exposure limit of 3.0 roentgens for the entire operation. Sampling pilots were permitted to receive up to 3.9 roentgens of gamma radiation (82; 91; 134).

• The exposure report of the 216th AFSWP Radiological Safety

Group listed the names, units, and total gamma doses for Joint AEC-DOD participants at TUMBLER-SNAPPER (22).

> • A widely publicized national call-in campaign sponsored by the Department of Defense has identified some of the nuclear weapons test participants.

6.2 SOURCES OF DOSIMETRY DATA

Most of the dosimetry data for Operation TUMBLER-SNAPPER were derived from film badge records. As stated in chapter 5, the AFSWP Radiological Safety Group maintained dosimetry records for each participant. **NOT TRUE**.

During 0peration TUMBLER-SNAPPER the film badge was the primary device used to measure 'the radiation dose received by individual participants. The film badge normally worn at chest level on the outside of clothing, was designed to measure the wearer's exposure to gamma radiation from external sources. The film badge was insensitive, however, to neutron radiation and did not measure the amount of radioactive material, if any, that might have been inhaled or ingested.

Radiological safety personnel issued, received, developed, nd interpreted film badges during Operation TUMBLER-SNAPPER. They recorded film badge data manually, maintaining a dosimetry record for each Participant. At the conclusion of the operation, all dose records for Desert Rock participants and all records indicating overexposure for AFSWP and scientific personnel were forwarded to their home stations. When the individual left the service his records were retired to a Federal records repository (91; 108).

On this page # 156 of report # ADA 122-242, you will notice in the sources of dosimetry data, It States;

"**MOST**" (and I have A real problem with this kind of word, when your health and care depend on the rest of this sentence.) We'll start again.

"**MOST**" of the dosimetry data for operation TUMBLER-SNAPPER were derived from film badge records." please let me ask where did the rest of the "dosimetry data" come from ? ? It goes on to say in the next sentence, "The AFSWP Radiological Safety Group maintained dosimetry records for each participant" now you know this is not true, because about 8 or 10 pages back, we Just covered shot Fox and learned from their own records that the A.E.C. only distributed 340 film badges, when they should have distributed 16,000 to 25,000, SO THIS IS AN OUTRIGHT DISTORTION OF FACTS. Well at any rate, it looks to me like **none** of this paragraph is the truth. So let's go to the next paragraph on this page, because it doesn't get any better than this.

This next paragraph, is at least partly true. "The film badge was the primary device used to measure the radiation dose received by individual participants. The film badge, normally, worn at chest level on the outside of the clothing." This is not true according to report DNA 6021F page #76 in this book. It

181

was worn in the chest pocket. (this is the truth) Now for the rest of the paragraph. "was designed to measure the wearers exposure to **GAMMA Radiation** from external sources. The film **badge was insensitive however, to NEUTRON Radiation** and did not measure the amount of radioactive material, if any, that **may have been ingested."** Now really, I can't imagine how the AEC could take this film badge reading as our accurate dosage, when we were out in the desert running in circles, swallowing and inhaling dust so thick, it would make you choke and cough.

I am sure that the people that wrote this was never involved in an Atomic test, or really never even read or studied an atomic explosion, or they wouldn't be dumb enough to try to convince us of some of the things we were Supposed to have done. However, if they can convince the public, they can take the compensation and healthcare, that we should have received. Then they can put it in their own pockets and call it wages, or job security.

One of the things that is happening is these greedy people don't tell the Government how much it's costing for their own wages AND EXPENSE ACCOUNTS. They only keep pointing a finger at us veterans and say. You can't give these veterans anything or you'll have to pay them millions. They have the U.S. Government believing them...

UNTIL THERE IS A CONGRESSIONAL INVESTIGATION INTO THE FILM BADGE DOSEAGE AND RECONSTRUCTION PROGRAM, AND TO DO STUDIES ON WHAT DISEASES BESIDES CANCER ARE CAUSED BY RADIATION WE WILL DIE IN VERY FEW YEARS AND THE GOVERNMENT WILL HAVE WON BY COVERUP.

6.3.2   Instances of Gamma Exposure Exceeding Established Limits

As stated in chapter 5, the gamma exposure limit for participants at TUMBLER-SNAPPER was 3.0 roentgens (108).

Cloud sampling pilots, however, were authorized to receive exposures up to 3.9 roentgens (82). Table 6-7 lists the units or organizations that included AEC-DOD personnel who received gamma exposures in excess of the established limits (22; 72; 142).

Several of the overexposed personnel listed in table 6-7 participated in Military Effects Test Group projects that required them to enter radiation areas to retrieve instruments and records. Some of these projects, with their fielding organizations, are:

· Project 2.1 (Signal Corps Engineering Laboratories)

· Project 6.1 (Bureau of Ships; Signal Corps Engineering Laboratories)
· Project 17.1 (Los Alamos Scientific Laboratory).

In addition, research indicates that the individual from the Army Chemical Center participated in Project 1.9, "Pre-shock Dust," and that the participant from the Engineer Research and Development Laboratories took part in Project 3.4, "Minefield Clearance."
Overexposures resulted from a variety of activities. For example, most personnel entered the test area at recovery hour or when permitted by the Test Manager, but personnel from Projects 1.9, 2.1, and 17.1 were permitted to enter the shot area before recovery hour because immediate recovery of equipment or data was necessary to ensure accurate results. Personnel from Project 3.4 inspected, recovered, and replaced land mines that had been placed around ground zero before the shot. To complete these activities personnel may have spent considerable time in radiation areas. Project 8.1 personnel tested various radiac instruments and survey techniques under field conditions, which
On page # 159 in report # 122-242 it talks about overexposure. we will cover some of the overexposed in another

183

few pages. what I would like to cover on this page is **WHY** the overexposures happened.

In paragraph 2 it states some of the overexposures, but the only ones they list here is laboratories that are really not on the test site. So it baffles me as to how they are included in this Tumbler-Snapper series. It takes some explanation to me on this. It does say a couple of outfits took part in the test, but I won't investigate this any further because I want to explain WHY we were overdosed, on this page.

In paragraph 3 at the bottom of the page I will go through a little at a time and tell you what they are saying. (in truth) It is saying that overexposures resulted from a variety of ways, however they are only going to tell us about one of the ways, instead of telling us about the variety of ways.

The one way of overexposure they are talking about is this. Most personnel enter the test area when they are permitted by the Test Manager to do so. How you can tell when "recovery hour" takes place is by the radiation monitors. (AFSWP OR THE 216th) We go out and monitor the area, and map the area. Some times this is done several times, and some times for several DAYS until the radiation "Isointensity Lines" are mapped and O.K."d by the Test Manager. When it is safe, then an AFSWP monitor will take the scientist in to recover their instruments. This is considered "Recovery Hour".

Personnel from some projects "were permitted to enter the shot area before recovery hour." (or before it was safe to enter) One thing you have to realize is the word "permitted" should be left out of this ENTIRELY, because if we had our way we would not have gone in until we had it safe. The word "**ORDERED**" **should replace permitted,** one reason was, we did only what we were told and the A.E.C. made sure we did not do anything more than we were "**ORDERED**".

It says, and here is the reason. "personnel were permitted to enter the shot area before recovery hour because immediate recovery of equipment or data was necessary to ensure accurate results.

184

So think about it. Were they really concerned about our safety, or were they more concerned about the data and test results. Some call us "Guinea Pigs" I call it authority abuse.

I will cover another sentence in this paragraph and it is pretty much of the same. It again is called authority abuse. It speaks for itself. "To complete- these activities personnel **MAY** have spent considerable time in radiation areas." what they are saying here is that they sent us in, KNOWING WE WERE GOING TO BE IN THERE TO LONG AND GET AN OVERDOSE OF RADIATION required them to enter radiation areas (22; 46; 72; 92; 116; 138; 142; 143; 151).

Members of the Radiological Safety Group provided radiological safety monitors for all shots. These monitors accompanied AFSWP project personnel on many of the recovery missions. In addition, radiological safety personnel surveyed the shot area after each detonation and manned the checkpoints to the radiation areas. Members of the Radiological Safety Group spent more time in or near radiation areas than other personnel, especially because-they repeated their activities during several shots. Personnel from the following units were members of the Radiological Safety Group at TUMBLER-SNAPPER (91):

·   AFSWP Test Command
·   Carswell AFB, Texas
·   Naval Air Station, North Island, California
·   216th Chemical Service Company.

The 4925th Test Group gathered radioactive samples from the clouds resulting from the detonations for analysis by personnel from various test projects. Because this task required the Pilots to fly near or through the clouds their potential exposures were increased (82; 88).

Documentation of the activities of the representatives from the Headquarters of the Armed Forces Special Weapons Project, Fort Belvoir, Fort McClellan, Indian Springs AFB, and the l009th Special Weapons Squadron was not found.

185

On page # 160, report # 122-242. This may be one of the most important papers, or statements in our study to prove that there was definitely a cover-up by the A.E.C. or a distortion of facts.

First of all, this page tells us which groups, in the test received the most radiation, and on the same page, tells us, "their records were not found." I can't believe that our Government would try to convince us that the records could be lost, on just those that received the most radiation, in the tests.

"Members of the Radiological safety group provided Radiological safety monitors for all shots." our "Monitors accompanied our personnel on many recovery missions." Also our group RAD-SAFE (AFSWP) "Surveyed the shot area after each detonation and manned the check points to the radiation areas. Members of the Radiological Safety Group spent more time in or near radiation areas than other personnel, especially because they repeated their activities during several shots."

Besides these four groups listed, another one of our AFSWP group is mentioned in the next paragraph, it says. "The 4925th test group gathered radioactive samples from the clouds." "Because this task required the Pilots (and Monitors) to fly near or through the clouds, their potential exposures were increased.

The 216th Chemical Service Company is listed with the, Afswp Test Command,

Carswell AFB, Texas, AND

Naval Air Station, North Island California, as outfits in the next paragraph.

"Documentation of the activities of AFSWP, FORT BELVOIR, FORT McCLELLAN, INDIAN SPRINGS AFB, and the 1009th AFSWP SQUADRON WAS NOT FOUND."

All of the way through these tests it shows how slip shod our tests were carried out. I will list a few of the errors in judgment or poor judgment that was used, in this book.

Table 6-2: DISTRIBUTION OF GAMMA RADIATION EXPOSURES FOR ARMY PERSONNEL AND AFFILIATES, OPERATION TUMBLER-SNAPPER

Units	Personnel Identified by Name	Personnel Identified by Name and by Film Badge	Average Gamma Exposure (Roentgens)	Gamma Exposure (Roentgens) <.1	.1-1.0	1.0-2.5	2.5-5.0	5.0+
Antiaircraft Artillery Detachment (Provisional)	11	0						
Army Chemical Center	3	3	2.463	0	0	1	1	0
Desert Rock IV	729	729	0.153	286	432	3	0	0
Edgewood Arsenal	3	3	1.949	0	0	3	3	0
Engineer Research and Development Laboratories	1	1	5.830	0	0	0	0	1
Fort Belvoir, VA	13	12	3.327	1	3	2	4	3
Fort McClellan, AL	4	4	4.613	0	0	2	1	1
Fort Monmouth, NJ	3	2	2.641	0	0	2	0	0
Observers	10	1	0.024	1	0	0	0	0
Radiation Safety	1	1	3.440	0	0	0	1	0
Sixth Army	54	0						
Sixth Army Special Field Chemical, Radiological and Biological School	47	0						
1st Armored Division	34	0						
1st Armored Division, 701st Armored Infantry Battalion	54	0						
11th Airborne Division	13	0						
18th Signal Operations Battalion	12	0						
31st Infantry Division (Dixie Division), Camp Atterbury, IN	18	0						
47th Infantry Division	26	0						
82nd Airborne Division	96	0						
216th Chemical Service Company	74	74	1.340	5	15	42	10	2
369th Engineer Amphibious Support Regiment	57	3	0.187	0	3	0	0	0
Other*	406	9	0.185	0	9	0	0	0
Unit Unknown**	136	6	0.185	0	6	0	0	0
TOTAL	1796	843	396	295	482	60	17	7

* For list of units in this category, see table 6-2a.

** Unit information unavailable.

128

Page # 162 of report # 122-242. This is a breakdown of radiation exposures for Army participants. It is hard to imagine how many of these people only had one badge for the whole 90 day test. It is also something to think about, when you think about having 10,600 total participants, and only 1803, at one time, had a film badge. Out of this total of 1,803, there was 843 of these were Army. In all the rest of the services and civilians added together there were only 960 total that were not in the Army.

We could go a step further and say out of the total of 843 from the Army, 729 of these were with Desert Rock, and only 9 Of them received low level radiation, and NONE of the 729 were overdosed.

IF there was 843 army and 729 were involved in a test, that leaves 114, of which 74 were in the 216th.

So only 40 film badges were distributed in the whole test. that is if you don't count the 729 in the desert rock test. and the 74 from the 216th.

Can you imagine out of the 10,600, that in 91 days and all of the errors in judgment being made, that **a ridiculously low overdose count for this whole test was only a total of 58.** (ON PAGE # 11 in report # 122-242)

It is almost unbelievable that there was only 58 total overdoses and the 216th had 20 % of them (12). When you look at all of the total Army outfits involved in the tests, there were only 61 that had 1.0 to 3.0 roentgens of radiation, which is the next step below being overdosed. Out of the whole Army, the 216th had 42 of the 61 in that category.

In other words if you add everyone in the Army together that had over 1.0 roentgens of radiation, the total is only 85 and the 216th had 54 0f them.

This would leave only 21 people in the Whole army that received over 1.0 roentgens.

Are you going to swallow figures like this ? ?

188

Table 6-7: FILM BADGE READINGS EXCEEDING ESTABLISHED LIMITS FOR DOD PARTICIPANTS AT TUMBLER-SNAPPER

Unit or Organization	Number of Personnel	Total Exposures (Roentgens)
Armed Forces Special Weapons Project	1	3.2
Armed Forces Special Weapons Project Test Command	7	3.0, 3.0, 3.1, 3.7, 4.2, 4.7, 6.1
Army Chemical Center	1	3.3
Carswell AFB, TX	1	4.5
Engineer Research and Development Laboratories	1	5.9
Fort Belvoir, VA	7	3.5, 3.6, 3.7, 4.8, 5.5, 6.9, 7.0
Fort McClellan, AL	2	3.2, 10.8
Indian Springs AFB, NV	2	3.2, 3.5
Naval Air Station, North Island, CA	1	4.2
Project 2.1 (Signal Corps Engineering Laboratories)	2	3.7, 3.9
Project 6.1 (Bureau of Ships; Signal Corps Engineering Laboratories)**	1	3.1
Project 7.4 (1009th Special Weapons Squadron)	1	3.5
Project 17.1 (Los Alamos Scientific Laboratory)	2	3.5, 3.9
Radiological Safety	1	3.4
216th Chemical Service Company	12	3.3, 3.3, 3.4, 3.4, 3.5, 3.6, 4.0, 4.0, 4.4, 4.9, 6.1, 8.0
4925th Test Group**	8	4.0, 4.1, 4.2, 4.2, 4.3, 4.8, 6.9, 7.6
TOTAL	50	

* Individual exposures are listed by name and project in the film badge records. Where two or more organizations fielded a project, specific organization of participation for an individual cannot be determined.

** Subject to 3.9 roentgen AFSWC limit.

130

U.S. Department of Commerce
National Technical Information Service
Operation Tumbler-Snapper 1952
Report # 60197 Page # 178
Accession # ADA 122-242

189

When you look at this graph, what can you say? I AM SPEECHLESS Does the A.E.C. really believe that they can convince us that black is really white, if you look at it long enough ? ?

The first thing this graph tells you is that out of a total of 12,600 personnel (their figures page # 1) the total amount of 50 personnel was all that was overdosed. If they can get you to believe that out of 8 tests, some more than twice as powerful as Hiroshima, Japan, that killed 80,000 people. Then to say that there was only 50 people overdosed.

Let's face it The A.E.C. must think that the radiation left us brain damaged also...

Let's go a step further, this graph tells you that the 216th had 25 % of the 50 personnel, (12) that were overdosed in this complete test, which is the whole Tumbler-Snapper series.

WE have to realize that we only had 74 film badges issued to us. Only being issued 74 film badges out of 138 men that we had on the test doesn't bother me near as bad as trying to figure out , how many of the 74 were reconstructed.

Then just try to imagine that 25 % of all of the personnel that were overdosed in the whole test, came out of 74 badges.

Another 8 overdosed comes out of the 197 men in "AFSWP," and 1 came from "Radiological Safety." This is a part of our group. So you can say 40 % of those overdosed on the whole test were from AFSWP. Or 21 of AFSWAP out of 50 were overdosed.

I think it is a disgrace that we didn't have more film badges, because a lot of the men that went into ground zero, on maneuvers, I'm positive got as much or more radiation than we did. But they didn't get any Film Badges at all, compared to the number of men involved.

I'm going to end this because we have waited our whole lives to see how the facts were covered up and the facts that are released are so distorted it will make you cry.

190

The Government has given our compensation to the ones researching these books, and reconstructing our dosage, and They come up with: Nothing from nothing is nothing, and that's what we get, while they are spending our medical help and compensation.

I am speaking for myself. While I can pass the means test, because I have nothing, and they gave what some Veterans deserve to these people that have distorted the facts so that they can have their yacht's.

AVAILABILITY INFORMATION

An availability statement has been included at the end of the reference citation for those readers who wish to read or obtain copies of source documents. Availability statements were correct at the time the bibliography was prepared. It is anticipated that many of the documents marked unavailable may become available during the declassification review process. The Coordination and Information Center (CIC) and the National Technical Information Service (NTIS) will be provided future DNA-WT documents bearing an EX after the report number.

Source documents bearing an availability statement of CIC may be reviewed at the following address:

Department of Energy
Coordination and Information Center
(Operated by Reynolds Electrical & Engineering Co., Inc.)
ATTN: Mr. Richard V. Nutley
2753 S. Highland
P.O. Box 14100   Phone: (702) 734-3194
Las Vegas, Nevada 89114 FTS: 598-3194

Source documents bearing an availability statement of NTIS may be purchased from the National Technical Information

Service. When ordering by mail or phone, please include both the price code and the NTIS number. The price code appears in parentheses before the NTIS order number.

> National Technical Information Service
> 5285 Port Royal Road   Phone: (703) 487-4650
> Springfield, Virginia 22161   (Sales Office)

Additional ordering information or assistance may be obtained by writing to the NTIS, Attention: Customer Service or by calling (703) 487-4660.

27. Armed Forces Special Weapons Project [Test Command]. "Weekly Activities Summary, Period Ending 28 March 1952." Washington, D.C. AFSWP. 28 March 1952. 3 Pages. ***

28. Armed Forces Special Weapons Project, Test Command. "Weekly Activities Summary for Period Ending 4 April 1952." Mercury, NV.: TC, AFSWP. 4 April 1952. 20 Pages. ***

29. Armed Forces Special Weapons Project, Test Command. "Weekly Activities Summary, Period Ending 25 April 1952." Mercury, NV.: TC, AFSWP. 25 April 1952. 15 Pages. ***

30. Armed Forces Special Weapons Project, Test Command. "Weekly Activities Summary, Period Ending 9 May 1952." Mercury, NV.: TC, AFSWP. 9 May 1952. 6 Pages. ***

31. Armed Forces Special Weapons Project, Test Command. "Weekly Activities Summary, Period Ending 30 May 1952." Mercury, NV.: TC, AFSWP. 30 May 1952.

12 Pages. ***

32. Armed Forces Special Weapons Project, Test Command, Deputy
    Commander. Letter to Deputy Test Director [Subject: manned Camera Positions for Shot 8.] Mercury, NV. 26 May 1952. 2 Pages. **

33. Armed Forces Special Weapons Project, Test Command, Military Effects Test Group. [File: Access Lists for TUMBLER-SNAPPER, 31 March--4 June 1952.] 1952.
    66 Pages. **

34. Arnold, Keith. "Effects of Atomic Explosions on Forest Fuels, Project 8.1." Washington, D.C.: AFSWP. WT-506. 1952. 35 Pages. ***

35. Aronson, C. J.; Moulton, J. F.; Petes, J.; et al. Free-Air and Ground-Level Pressures Measurements, Projects 1.3 and 1.5. Washington, D.C.: Headquarters, AFSWP. WT-513-EX. March 1980. 254 Pages. (All) AD/A995 029. *

    *Available from NTIS; order number appears before the asterisk.
    **Available at CIC.
    ***Not available, see Availability Information page.
    ****Requests subject to Privacy Act restrictions.

Page 180. . Availability of documents on Nuclear Testing.

Page 184..Article ~ 31 "Weekly Activities Summary, period ending May 30, 1952, Mercury, Nevada. TC AFSWP 30 May 1952, 12 pages."

If it is possible to have this document released from "Top Secret" to "Public Information." I could prove the things I have said about Shot Fox and how carelessly the film badges and records were kept, throughout the whole Tumbler-Snapper test. These records would confirm the earlier story I have written about the evacuation of Groom Mine. It would also prove that there was a lot of problems that were never released to the public..

I think that the reason these records were never released is not because it was "confidential", but the records will show the following errors.

"It was not adverse weather conditions that delayed this shot 12 days, but **this shot was a "DUD".** Errors alone were to blame. Two men alone walked several days across the desert lifting the wires out of the ground, trying to locate a broken wire. The AEC thought the reason the bomb did not go off was a broken wire. When the two men got to the base of the tower, and the wires were still in tact, they realized it had to be something on the tower or bomb. The AEC thought at this time it may be a stuck relay, and may detonate itself with the wind blowing. When the men climbed the 300 foot tall tower, they found the problem was, the wires were never hooked to the detonator of the bomb itself.

WHAT A TERRIBLE ERROR WITH 10,000 LIVES COUNTING ON A PERSON WHO DID NOT DOUBLE CHECK OR HAD NO SUPERVISING BACKUP.

There were a lot more errors on shot Fox that you will read about in this book. The largest cover-up on Shot Fox was, how many conflicting stories there are in this book about the amount of personnel that were present, and what their duties were in this Shot. I will cover this at another time in this book.

DNA 6020F

SHOTS
ABLE, BAKER, CHARLIE, AND DOG

The First Tests of the
TUMBLER-SNAPPER Series
1 APRIL - 1 MAY 1952

DTIC
SELECTED
DEC 1 0 1982

A

United States Atmospheric Nuclear Weapons Tests
Nuclear Test Personnel Review

Prepared by the Defense Nuclear Agency as Executive Agency
for the Department of Defense

135

This is a good description of what it is like to watch an Atom Bomb detonation in the desert. I can not add much to this except that it was dropped from a airplane and detonated at a height of 3,447 feet above the desert floor, .at 9:30 A.M.. The higher detonation causes more damage, because of the power loss when the force is knocking over buildings. This bomb was the largest or most powerful bomb ever dropped to this date of Apr.22, 1952.

Charlie was equal to	31,000 tons of T.N.T.
Hiroshima was equal to	15,000 tons of T.N.T.
Nagasaki was equal to	21,000 tons of T.N.T.

News nob was approximately 15 miles to Shot Charlie Ground Zero.

The sad part of it is the observers watching the detonation of the bomb didn't know it, but when they were swallowing the dirt, they were also swallowing RADIATION. The military personnel swallowed this dirt, every day that they worked in the desert.

One observer at News Nob described CHARLIE, shortly after detonation, as follows:

It was possible to discern the outline of the fireball, the rocket trails and the antiaircraft smoke puffs, although the light was near blinding. It appeared the sky behind the bomb was a deep red with white rocket lines etched on it ....

The cloud left a white vapor trail as it rose, there was no mushroom stem as ordinarily occurs in low level bursts. This, combined with the high yield, gave an unusually clean and spectacular atomic cloud. The cloud formed its customary doughnut in which the brown oxides of nitrogen were clearly visible. The cloud retained its clear identity for perhaps five minutes.

The noise hurt my ears and of course the dust carried by the blast blotted out everything beyond a yard for a minute or so. The Desert Rock Master of Ceremonies had repeatedly warned the observers of the dust storm which would follow the blast, yet many individuals were so impressed by the first sight of the fireball that they were standing with their mouths wide open. Consequently when the blast wave arrived these persons received a mouth full of dust as their second impression of the atomic detonation.

Some observers stated that they could see the dust from the blast rolling towards their position (16).

CHARLIE. These troops then advanced to a position 6,400 meters south of ground zero. Meanwhile, a company of paratroopers was dropped behind enemy lines to sever enemy communications. The ground forces met at a location near ground zero to capture the enemy objective (42; 73; 75).

Participating troops reported to Camp Desert Rock by 18 April 1952. From 19 April to 21 April, the Instructor Group briefed them on the effects of a nuclear detonation and on radiological safety procedures. On 19 April, the troops rehearsed shot-day activities, including an inspection of the equipment display area (16; 42; 75).

HumRRO and ORO began their study during the preshot orientation period. On 19 April, HumRRO and ORO monitors tested 20 enlisted men from the 135th Infantry Regiment, 47th Infantry Division, and 19 enlisted men from the 504th Airborne Infantry Regiment, 82nd Airborne Division. They administered a polygraph test to these troops to determine their psychological responses to the maneuver in which they were to participate. On 21 April, HumRRO and ORO personnel conducted a rifle disassembly-assembly test, with 50 soldiers from the 165th Regiment, 31st Infantry Division, and 49 from the 504th Airborne Infantry Regiment, 82nd Airborne Division, participating.: The rifle test was repeated. immediately after the shot to determine 'if the physical responses of the troops were slower after they had witnessed a nuclear detonation for the first time (25; 77; 113).

At 0454 hours on 22 April, the troops, carrying rifles and wearing fatigue uniforms and steel helmets, began leaving Camp

Desert Rock for the trench area. They reached the trenches in a truck convoy by about 0815 hours. Before and after shot-time, a Desert Rock instructor briefed them, as described in section 4.1.2 of this chapter (69; 75; 95). at about 1105 hours and established an orbiting pattern. The paratroopers were to start parachuting at 1115 hours into the area north-northwest of ground zero, shown in figure 4-2. Figure 4-7 shows the paratroopers awaiting the signal to jump. At 1109 hours, the paratroopers in one C-46 began their jump, landing as far as 13 kilometers from the designated drop **zone.** Soon after, ;hey notified the pilot that five paratroopers had been injured on landing. At 1120 hours, the crew of this C-46 reported to the Air Operations Center that its paratroopers had jumped prematurely and the pilot asked the Air Operations Center to send a helicopter to assist the injured personnel. At 1141 hours, a YH-12 helicopter was dispatched from the Control Point. The YH-12 crew reported to the Air Operations Center at 1151 hours that the paratroopers' injuries were minor. An ambulance returned the injured paratroopers to Camp Desert Rock for medical attention (3-5; 57; 75).

Paratroopers in the other four aircraft jumped as scheduled. By 1120, they were either in descent or just reaching the ground. Figure 4-8 shows paratroopers descending over the designated drop zone. By about 1125, the aircraft left the shot area for the Yucca Lake airstrip, which they reached at 1143 hours (3-5; 57).

The paratroopers who landed in the designated drop zone probably marched south to meet the maneuver troops and service observers. This completed the maneuver. The ground troops, service observers, and paratroopers walked back to the parking area near the BJY to be monitored for radiation. According to the Schedule of Events, they were to leave the parking area at approximately :330 hours and travel in a truck convoy south on Mercury Highway, reaching Camp Desert Rock between 1500 and 1530 hours (95).

After the troops returned to Camp Desert Rock on shot-day, HumRRO and ORO monitors readministered the polygraph test.

Pages 97 & 101 Report DNA 6020F :

Shot Charlie on the April 22, 1952, The most powerful shot of the test is almost word for word like shot Fox on pages 89-90 on report # DNA 6021F. With no protective clothing at all, and this was another exercise to ground zero.

"The troops carrying rifles and wearing fatigue uniforms and steel helmets, began leaving Camp Desert Rock for the trench area." The so called "protective clothing" was more of a joke than anything of any value to the troops, there were many tests given to the troops such as, polygraph tests, psychological tests, rifle disassembly and assembly, before and after the shot and physical responses.

Page 101 report # DNA 6020F :

This page and mission is another goof-up, as was the rest of the whole project. When these paratroopers are in the plane getting ready to jump, a warning light (red) will go on in the airplane, this light gives the paratrooper six minutes to get ready to jump. Then the green light goes on to start jumping. The red light went on and the officer on one of the C-46's ordered his men to bail out over the mountains, 6 minutes early. The plane was in a full clime to gain altitude, for their glide pattern to drop the paratroopers. The troops on the ground said that the chutes opening sounded like artillery shots exploding. We could hear on the radios that there was an awful mess up in the mountains, and they were having trouble getting up to the injured troops. We heard that there were many many injured, but I guess we'll never know the truth.

Eleven minutes after the troops had jumped, the pilot radioed control point to send a helicopter to bring out the injured paratroopers. 32 minutes after the drop the helicopter got off the ground at control point, and 42 minutes after the drop, the helicopter arrived at the scene of the injured.

If you look at the map and see how close the paratroopers were dropped to Ground Zero on shot Charlie, you might then realize that the troopers that were dropped up in the mountains were the lucky ones.

Project 4.3, Biological Effectiveness of Neutron Radiation from Nuclear Weapons, was conducted by the Naval Radiological Defense Laboratory to study the biological effects of neutron radiation on mice. At about 1900 hours the evening before the detonation, eight participants in two weapons carriers began placing approximately 30 mice in mouse cages at each field station. They spent about one hour in this assignment. The stations, which were shielded with lead, bismuth, or aluminum, were approximately 780 to 1,330 meters from ground Zero (35; 95).

After the area was opened for recovery operations, 12 participants spent about 30 minutes retrieving the mice. To determine the effects of neutron radiation on the mice, project participants performed a pathological examination of the animals in the laboratory (35; 95).

Project 4.4, Gamma Depth Dose Measurement in Unit Density Material, was performed by the Naval Medical Research Institute. The experiment was designed to improve techniques used to evaluate biological effects of radiation on living tissue, particularly of the human body. To measure initial and residual gamma doses, project participants placed dosimeters inside lucite spheres, which approximated the density of human tissue. Before the detonation, personnel placed nine spheres on A-frames located about 1,140 to 1,690 meters south of ground zero. After recovery hour was declared, seven personnel in a weapons carrier and a pickup truck spent about one hour retrieving the spheres (36; 95).

Project 4.5, Flash Blindness, was conducted by the Air Force School of Aviation Medicine, with assistance from the Air Training Command, SAC, and Brooke Army Medical Center. The project was to determine how much the flash of a nuclear detonation impairs night vision. The protection afforded by the use of protective goggles was also evaluated (33; 38; 111).

Two hours before the shot, 27 personnel traveled by bus to a trailer near the Control point at Yucca pass, approximately 16 kilometers from the intended ground zero, to witness the detonation. Project procedure required participants to adapt their eyes to darkness by wearing dark goggles for 30 minutes and then by remaining in the darkened trailer for another 30 minutes before the detonation.

Along the side of the trailer were 12 portholes fitted with shutters for exposing the eyes of the test subjects to the nuclear flash. The shutters opened 48 milliseconds after the detonation and closed two seconds later. During the exposure, half of the subjects wore protective red goggles. After the exposure, participants were required to read lighted instruments to determine how soon after exposure a person could see well enough to perform assigned tasks. Various instruments were used to examine the subjects' vision after exposure (33; 38; 95; 111).

Project 4,6, Time Course of Thermal Radiation as Measured by Burns in Pigs, was conducted by the Naval Medical Research Institute and the University of Rochester Atomic Energy Project. The Naval Medical Research institute provided equipment, while the Atomic Energy Project supplied the test animals and conducted the biological experiments. The project was designed to study the biological effects of thermal radiation on pigs (79).

On the day before the detonation, project personnel weighed the pigs and inspected their skin for disease or injury. From five to three hours before the detonation, nine project participants transported the pigs to stations 1,070, 1,280, 1,550. and 2.370

meters from ground zero. After anesthetizing the pigs and placing them in containers, the men left the shot area.

About two hours after the detonation, four men in a truck began recovering the animals and inspecting their containers to

Page 167-168 of report # DNA 6020F :

This is another article on another, of several eye tests, or Guinea Pig tests with the Military Personnel. This test is described in a little more detail than the other tests, but it doesn't tell you the rest of the story.

The notes on this experiment said, "The project was terminated after Shot 4 in order to evaluate the significance of lesions of the retina which were produced in two of the subjects."

I would like to bring out some of the errors in judgment that were ordered and carried out in these tests.

1. Eye tests   page 92 6019F, 167-168 6020F
2. Lost our radiation dosage records   page 160 6019F
3. 1st shot less than 10 miles from camp the outer 7 shots were 40 miles away. we drove within 3 miles of Ground Zero, every day going to and coming home from work, without film badges
                    page 10 6019F
4.   No protective clothing, photo   page 69-71 6019F
5.   Orientation instructors failed   page 128-9 6019F
6.   Film badges insensitive (no good)   page 156 6019F
7.   Overexposure to radiation on purpose   page 159 6019F
8.   Do the Job at the cost of overdose   page 42 6021F
9.   An atomic bomb a DUD (unbelievable)   page 48 6021F
10. Troops marched to Ground Zero without protective clothing and film badges   page 11 6019F
11. To decontaminate, brushed with brooms page 77 6021F
12. Sent men into Groom Mine after the civilians were evacuated.
13. Sent in Paul Martin with poor equip, and forgot he was there (poor management)   page 142 6021F

14. Physical response experiments   page 97 6020F
15. Error in judgment again paratroopers ordered to jump prematurely, and the rest to close to G.Z.   page 101 6020F
16. Every one was overdosed by the end of the test. see letter by Richard Hallen. never drove an army vehicle, but everyone was overdosed and no alternative, see his letter
17. On the last shot Wally Holland was ordered to drive to Ground Zero, as a monitor even though he had failed the driving test the day prior to the last shot. The reason he was sent in was because everyone else was overdosed. See his letter.

I could write for hours about what went wrong on these tests, but I think by now you already know, so I won't waste your time. One thing I would like to add is, all of the questionnaires were sent out at the same time to every part of the United States so not one of these men knew what the others were writing about. some of these men have not seen each other for many, many years and they wrote down only what happened to themselves.

Radiochemical and Physical Analysis of Atomic Bomb Debris, and for Program 13, Radiochemistry Sampling. Two other T-33s aborted their missions shortly after leaving Indian Springs AFB. A B-29 sampler control aircraft, with an AFSWC aircrew and a LASL scientific advisor onboard, directed the operations of the sampler aircraft. The samplers flew at altitudes of 31,000 to 33,000 feet and made a total of 17 penetrations of the cloud.

The following listing details their activities (1-3; 36; 37; 52; 69):

AIRCRAFT TYPE AND TAIL NUMBER	TAKEOFF TIME	TOTAL TIME IN CLOUD (seconds)	TOTAL DOSIMETER READING (roentgens)	LANDING TIME
Sampler ControlB-29.				
(386)	0350			1030
B-29 (285)	0400	NR*	0.675	0925

T-33 (920)	0535	NR	0.700	0725
T-33 (048)	0526	NR	NR	0625
T-SS (913)	0535	NH	0.440	0725
F-84 (040)	0558	NR	0.050	0815
F-84 (054)	0605	120	0.030	0735
F-84 (043)	0608	NR	NR	0735
F-84 (042)	0610	NR	O. 8OO	0745

*NR indicates not reported.

On completing their mission, the samplers returned to Indian Springs AFB and parked in the northeast corner of the parking area. Pilots then shut down the engines and opened the aircraft canopies. The 3-29 crew's left the aircraft through the rear door between the stabilizer and the wing. The T-33 and F-84 crews

The following information is from a different report on the same test, but it reinforces the earlier issues.
U.S. Department Of Commerce
Report # 6021F - Accession # ADA 122-240
Tumbler-Snapper Series - 1952

Page 40 Looking at this Cloud Sampling Mission Report you will very easily see how the facts are distorted. For example only one of the nine Aircraft listed, has listed the amount of time it was in the cloud and this plane was recorded with the least radiation. The time in the Radiation cloud has absolutely no bearing on how long this plane carried the radiation, or dosage
Assuming the first B-29 listed in the report (tail # 386) took off at 3:50 A.M. and landed at 10:30 A.M., or they spent 6 hours and 40 minutes, and had absolutely no information on anything, including the amount of radiation they received during the flight. Please ask yourself, "what was the purpose of sampling the Radioactive clouds and finish the test and have absolutely no information." Or was it so high that the AEC wanted to misplace the results of the test. Ask another Question "If this test was

important enough to do wasn't it important enough to take care of the records to produce some kind of conclusions to whatever experiments they were trying to resolve?" I guess this is just one of those orders. "Don't complicate the experiment with the answers."

I look at the second one, another B-29 Tail #285 that was in the air 5 hours and 25 minutes with almost .7 Roentgens of radiation. if the plane found the cloud as soon as it got in the air, and speed is essential for all missions and tests, it would have accumulated 3.8 Roentgens. This amount of radiation would have overdosed the whole crew for the whole year in just these 5 1/2 hours.

The only thing you really learn while looking at this experiment is that all of the information has been eradicated. This is another Guessing Game. You know the take off and landing time, but **personnel's radiation dosage is figured on a time and dosage ratio.**

In other words if you have a dosage of 2.0 (TWO) Roentgens per hour for a time period of 3 hours, then you have to multiply the 2.0 Roentgens times the 3 hours and you then have a film badge reading or a personal dosage on your record of 6.0 (SIX) Roentgens. which means that you have twice the legal allowable dosage for 1 (ONE) year, because you are only allowed 3.0 Roentgens per year.

The thing that bothers me the most, after spending 91 days working on 8 tests, the **AEC thinks we're dumb enough to believe these "so called facts."** Are they laughing at us in our face?

Aerial Surveys of Terrain

After the detonation, two C-47s and one L-20, based at Indian Springs AFB, conducted radiological surveys of the onsite and offsite terrain. One C-47 (tail number 386) left at 0530 hours, flew at heights of 700 to 5,000 feet, and returned at

1200 hours. The other C-47 (tail number 308) left at 0715 hours, conducted its survey at an altitude of 10,000 feet, and returned at 1230 hours. The L-20 (tail number 464) left at an undesignated time, conducted its survey at 1,000 to 7,500 feet above the terrain, and landed at an unreported time (1-3; *36;* 37; 52; 69).

2.3 RADIATION PROTECTION AT SHOT EASY

The main purpose of the radiation protection procedures developed by the test groups and AFSWC for Operation TUMBLER-SNAPPER was to keep individual exposures to ionizing radiation to a minimum, while still allowing participants to accomplish their missions.

Logistics and Materiel

During the period 7 May to 24 May 1952, which covered the 7 May detonation of Shot EASY, the Logistics and Materiel Department issued about 525 film badges to test group personnel (both DOD and AEC personnel are included in this group). The department also issued 1,174 sets of protective clothing and 253 radiation survey instruments (43).

Monitoring

The initial ground radiation survey began at 0522 hours, slightly more than an hour after the detonation, and continued until 0650 hours. Because of the relatively large radiation area and the rough terrain, it was not possible to complete the survey, as indicated in figure 2-3. The closest that the initial

Page 42   **DNA 6021 F**

Rather than photocopy the page for proof I'll just quote it and give my opinion on this same page.

Article 2.3 RADIATION PROTECTION AT SHOT EASY:

"The main purpose of the Radiation Protection procedures developed by the test groups and a AFSWC for Operation TUMBLER-SNAPPER was to keep individual exposures to Ionizing radiation to a minimum, while still allowing participants to accomplish their missions."

To look at this a little closer, it states in the last sentence that the <u>AEC will still allow the participants to accomplish their work.</u> In other words the AEC will keep the ionizing radiation to as low as they can, but if it comes to getting the mission done or not getting it done, the personnel may get overdosed, <u>but the mission will get done.</u>

Let's go back a few pages to Page 159 in the preceding report ADA 122-242 and I'll quote a couple of lines, that will show you that <u>the mission will be completed at any cost.</u>

PAGE 159 ADA 122 242.

"Several of the overexposed personnel participated in Military Effects Test Group Projects that required them to enter radiation areas to retrieve instruments and records."

"Overexposure resulted from a variety of activities. For example, <u>most</u> personnel entered the test area at RECOVERY HOUR or WHEN PERMITTED BY THE TEST MANAGER, but some personnel were permitted TO ENTER THE SHOT AREA BEFORE RECOVERY HOUR BECAUSE IMMEDIATE RECOVERY OF EQUIPMENT OR DATA WAS NECESSARY TO ENSURE ACCURATE RESULTS. To complete these activities, personnel may have spent considerable time in radiation areas."

Now please go to the top of this page and re-read the first paragraph, or Page # 42. Now do you believe that the AEC really tried to keep ionizing radiation to a minimum, when it came to getting the mission completed ? ?

SHOT FOX

Shot. FOX, as detonated with a yield of 11 kilotons at 0400 hours Pacific Standard Time on 25 May 1952. FOX, the sixth nuclear test of Operation TUMBLER-SNAPPER, was originally scheduled for 13'May 1952 but was rescheduled' for 25 May because of a misfiring of the device and adverse weather conditions. Shot FOX, a weapons development test, was part of the SNAPPER phase of Operation TUMBLER-SNAPPER. Developed by the Los Alamos scientific Laboratory, the FOX device was detonated on a 300-foot tower in Area 4 of Yucca Flat, UTM coordinates 795056. The Shot FOX cloud reached a height of about 41,000 feet and drifted east into Utah (1; 2; 8; 30; 31; 40; 67).

3.1 EXERCISE DESERT ROCK IV OPERATIONS AT SHOT FOX

Approximately 1,450 military observers participated in Desert Rock IV programs at Shot FOX. Camp Desert Rock support troops provided radiological safety, transportation, communications, and control functions for the observers in the forward area. No tactical troop maneuver was conducted at the shot (11; 12; 15; 50; 51; 58).

3.1.1 Participation of Camp Desert Rock Support Troops

In providing support for the observer program, the Camp Desert Rock troops sometimes entered the forward area. Two special staff sections, the Desert Rock Radiological Safety

Group and the Instructor Group, were particularly involved in shot-day operations.

The Desert Rock Radiological Safety Group implemented radiological safety procedures and was assisted by the AFSWP Radiological Safety Group in radiation surveys. Each survey team consisted of one driver, or a radio operator, and one radiological safety monitor from the Radiological Safety Group. An AFSWP radiological safety team accompanied Companies A, B, C, and D of the 701st Armored Infantry Battalian into the forward area. The 701st provided additional radiological monitoring for its units that went into the shot area (49; 51; 53).

The Instructor Group consisted of AFSWP personnel who replaced the less experienced Army personnel used at Shots CHARLIE and DOG. After the detonation, the instructors led observers through the display area to view the damage. They noted differences between the predicted and actual effects of the burst (51).

In addition to the Instructor. Group and the Desert Rock Radiological Safety Group, several other Desert Rock support elements participated in activities at Shot FOX.

Before the shot, personnel from the 369th Engineer Amphibious Support Regiment spent several days in the equipment display area placing military vehicles and ordnance at various distances from ground zero. Observers compared the preshot and postshot condition of these displays (49; 51).

The 31st and 23rd Transportation Truck Companies transported military personnel to and from the forward area. At shot-time, the vehicles were parked about 1,000 meters south of the observer trenches (49; 51).

The Desert Rock Signal Detachment established wire and radio communications within the forward area, as well as at Camp Desert Rock. After the shot, signal personnel operated the two mobile

Page 48 and 49 DNA 6021F

We have pretty well covered "Shot Fox", however, this page is the proof that the AEC is trying to make you believe that some adverse weather conditions were the cause of the delay, rather than the truth..IT WAS A DUD AND SOMEONE GOOFED on back-up checkups. Well we won't go into this again, but I wanted to go into some other inconsistencies on these two pages.

Paragraph # 2 Says "approximately 1,450 military observers participated in Desert Rock IV programs" "NO tactical troop maneuver was conducted at this shot." In the very first paragraph on the following page "49", it is recorded. "An AFSWP radiological safety team accompanied companies A, B, C, and D of the 701st Armored Infantry Battalion into the forward area."

In these 4 pages 48, 49, 50, and 52 the AEC says there was 1,450 troops in this test, I will put in an article of unknown origin. It is about the statements of Lt. Gen. Joseph M. Swing.

"The exercise is under the overall direction of Leut. Gen. Joseph M. Swing, Sixth Army Commanding General." He states that, "The Army contingent will include two battalion combat teams and supporting service troops and individual observers from stations in all parts of the United States, totaling about 4,500 participating in the series of tests,"

"The Navy" he said "will participate with 2 Marine battalion combat teams which, with observers, will total about 2,100."

"The Air Force representation will include Two flight units and observers with an overall total of approximately 500."

While we were stationed, and worked at Mercury, Nevada, we all (138 of the 216th) were told that on this one test there were 3,000 troops alone, hauled into the forward area before the shot and after the exercise were picked up and hauled out with military vehicles.

In paragraph two, page 50, the report says, "The medical detachment provided medical support in the forward area and at Camp Desert Rock. One doctor and six enlisted men set up an

210

aid station in the parking area south of the trenches and remained there throughout the exercise."

In the fifth paragraph on page 50 you will notice psycological tests were given.

Why is Cancer the only casualty in radiation, when personnel not connected to radiation, have psycological and a lot of other problems.

Public address systems in the display area to assist the Instructor Group in its presentations (49; 51).

The medical detachment provided medical support in the forward area and at Camp Desert Rock. One doctor and six enlisted men set up an aid station in the parking area south of the trenches and remained there throughout the exercise (49; 51).

During the shot-day activities, nine officers and 39 enlisted men from Company A, 505th Military Police Battalion, maintained traffic control for Desert Rock convoys in the forward area of the test site and at the FOX trench area (49; 51).

3.1.2 Troop Observer Activities

The observers at FOX consisted of 950 soldiers from the 701st Armored Infantry Battalion, 1st Armored Division, from Fort Hood, Texas, and an additional 500 participants from the continental armies and service schools (15).

Two Army contractors, the Human Resources Research Office (HumRRO) of George Washington University and the Operations Research Office (ORO) of Johns Hopkins University, conducted psychological tests on 670 of the observers from the 701st Armored Infantry Battalion. The general objective of these studies was to evaluate the participants' psychological reactions to various aspects of their Desert Rock IV experience. These psychological tests were a continuation of similar studies conducted by HumRRO and ORO at Exercise Desert Rock I daring Operation BUSTER-JANGLE in 1951 (53).

At TUMBLER-SNAPPER, HumRRO and ORO research was conducted mainly at Shots CHARLIE, FOX, and GEORGE. In particular, the experiments were designed to gather data on (17; 51; 53; 78):

In months preceding the Desert Rock IV maneuver, the "indoctrinated troops" were instructed on chemical, biological, and radiological topics at their home stations. At Camp Desert Rock, these troops were given an additional four hours of special indoctrination in nuclear effects. <u>The "briefed troops" at their bases. At Shot FOX, both the "indoctrinated troops" and "briefed troops" took part in the psychological tests at the Nevada Proving Ground. The "nonparticipants" remained at Fort Hood</u> throughout the Desert Rock IV exercises and were given psychological tests before, during, and after the Desert Rock maneuver.

Troops from Companies A, B, C, and D of the 701st left Fort Hood by train on 20 May 1952. They arrived at Camp Desert Rock on 22 May 1952. On 23 May, <u>Companies A, B, and C attended four one hour indoctrination lectures on bomb effects and on the previous TUMBLER-SNAPER detonations (53).</u>

On 24 May 1952, at 1120 hours, Companies A, B, C, and D boarded trucks at Camp Desert Rock and traveled to the FOX shot area to practice their shot-day activities. While in the trench area, shown in figure 3-1, these troops were briefed on what to expect at the detonation and the specific precautions to take during the nuclear test. This onsite briefing also included an inspection of the equipment display area and a drill using an artillery shell fired to simulate the FOX detonation. Following these activities, the troops returned to Camp Desert Rock and underwent psychological testing from 2000 to 2200 hours (49; 51).

At about 0050 hours on 25 May, the entire 701st Armored Infantry Battalion again moved by truck convoy from Camp Desert Rock to the shot area. The convoy proceeded north along Mercury Highway to the FOX trench area, arriving at about 0220 hours. The trenches, located in Area 1, were about 6,400 meters from ground zero. The troops went to their trenches, and the Instructor Group used the public address system to conduct a 30-minute preshot briefing, similar to that given during the practice on the previous day. The troops participating in this maneuver wore fatigue uniforms, web belts with canteens, and combat boots and film badges. They carried rifles and protective masks (48; 49).

At 0345 hours, 15 minutes before the detonation, the HumRRO and ORO monitors began administering the sweat tests to 248 men. At 0350 hours, the troops were ordered to enter the trencher. Then at 0356, HumRRO and ORO monitors administered another sweat tests to selected individuals. At 0358 hours, all personnel were given the two-minute warning for the-shot. "Troops were ordered to crouch below ground level and await the order to stand up following the detonation (17; 48; 49; 53; 78).

At 0400 hours the FOX device was detonated as planned, and five seconds later a Desert Rock instructor gave the command over the public address system for the troops to rise in the trenches. Twenty seconds after the detonation, the blast wave passed over the observer trenches. Soon after, all troops participating in the sweat test were directed to hand in instruments to the monitors (17; 48; 49; 53; 78).

Selected troops performed the rifle disassembly-assembly task at the trench area, probably in the first few minutes after the detonation. At 0415 hours, the HumRRO and ORO monitors gave the troops in the trench area a brief psychological test, consisting of a questionnaire about their reactions to the detonation. Meanwhile, AFSWP and Desert Rock radiological safety monitors went forward to survey the shot area.

At about 0630 hours, when the area was declared radiologically safe for operations, troops boarded the trucks, which had been brought to the trench area. The troops were then taken to the shot area to view the damage to the equipment displays, located southwest of ground zero, as shown in figure 3-1. The trucks were parked in a predesignated area southwest of

213

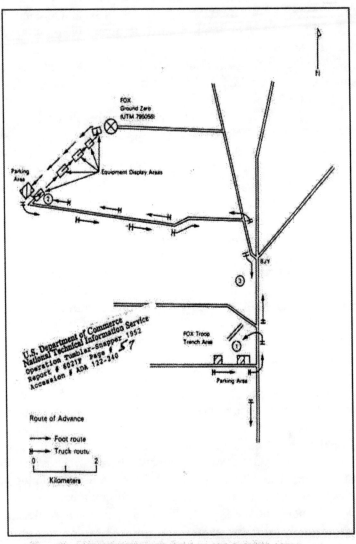

Figure 3-1: OBSERVER TRENCHES, DISPLAY AND PARKING AREAS,
AND ROUTES OF ADVANCE FOR EXERCISE DESERT ROCK IV
ACTIVITIES AT SHOT FOX

214

the equipment display, and the troops walked to the displays with radiological safety monitors from Camp Desert Rock in the lead. Army Chemical, Biological, and Radiological (CBR) monitors, without AFSWP supervision, surveyed the approach route to the equipment display. At the equipment displays, Instructor Group personnel Used the public address systems and loudspeakers posted throughout the area to comment on the damage caused by the detonation (17; 48; 49; 53; 78).

After viewing the equipment displays, the troops returned to the truck parking area for the trip to Camp Desert Rock. The troops probably left the parking area at 0930 hours for Camp Desert Rock, which they reached by 1130 hours. Beginning at 1400 hours, HumRRO and ORO monitors gave the troops a postshot psycho-logical test, consisting of a questionnaire.

The next day at 0500 hours, troops were given a second sweat test to compare the data obtained during the nuclear detonation with data obtained from the same troops in a less stressful situation. At 0900 hours, monitors gave a "volunteer" test, in which the troops were asked if they would like to participate in another nuclear weapons maneuver.

On 28 May 1952, the 701st Armored Infantry Battalion began its return to Fort Hood, arriving there on 30 May. At Fort Hood, the monitor teams continued to conduct psychological testing from 3 to 16 June 1952, when the HumRRO and ORO experiment was Completed (17; 47-49; 51; 53; 78). hours after the declaration of recovery hour, four men drove by truck into the area to retrieve film packets. They recovered the film farthest from ground zero and then worked their way toward ground zero. This task was scheduled to take three hours. Information gained from the film was eventually shared with Projects 1.13, 3.1, and 6.1; the Office, Chief of Army Field Forces; and the Marine Corps (57; 63).

Project 2.2, Gamma Ray Energy Spectrum of Residual Contamination, was conducted by the Signal Corps Engineering Laboratories. The objective was to determine the relative dose contribution of various gamma radiation energies in radiation areas following a nuclear detonation. Project personnel used radiation survey meters that had been modified to shield portions of the gamma ray energy spectrum. The information gained was to be used to determine the radiation exposure potential in test areas and to design survey instruments (77).

Before the shot, project personnel calibrated five AN/PDR-T1B radiac instruments. After the Test Manager announced recovery hour, participants placed the instruments in the shot area 3.5 feet above the ground on wooden tripods facing ground zero. About three hours after the burst, personnel took the first set of radiac instrument readings. At 1,450 meters from ground zero, the intensity was 1.2 R/h. At 3,000 meters from ground zero, the intensity was 0.02 R/h. The day after the shot, personnel returned to the shot area to take more gamma spectral readings. The first reading was taken at about 650 meters from ground zero, where the intensity was 1.09 R/h. Personnel made four other measurements that day at distances up to 1,290 meters from ground zero. Two days after the detonation, Project 2.2 personnel again entered the test area to take another set of gamma energy spectral measurements. The highest intensity, 0.22 R/h, was measured 650 meters from ground zero (63; 77).

Project 6.1, Evaluation of Military Radiac Equipment, was conducted by the Bureau of Ships and the Signal Corps Engineering Laboratories. The objective was to evaluate rediac survey and dose-alarm equipment, dosimeters, and the instruments and techniques used for rapid aerial surveys. Two hours after recovery hour, six project personnel in one vehicle spent three hours recovering dosimeters from radial lines 910 to 2,740 meters east of ground zero. At 0900 hours on the day after the detonation, eight personnel in two vehicles cook new readings where the radiation intensity vas 8.0 R/h. In addition, Project 6.1 personnel furnished standard and[L] experimental radiation survey instruments to other projects so that the instruments could be evaluated (63; 72).

Project 6.3, Evaluation of a Filtration System for Pressurized Aircraft, was conducted by the Army Chemical Center. The objective was to determine the adequacy of a system for filtering particulate airborne fission products from the cabin air supply of a B-29 aircraft. Air samples taken before and after passing through the filtering unit were compared for levels of radio-activity. The results showed that the filter unit removed more than 99.9 percent of the airborne fission products from the air stream entering the unit (66).

The 4925th Test Group (Atomic) provided the two B-29 aircraft that participated in this project. After five cloud penetrations at altitudes ranging from 30,000 to 33,000 feet, the aircraft returned to Indian Springs AFB. The filter samples were then removed from the B-29s and transported by B-25 courier air-craft to the Army Chemical Center (36; 63; 66). Courier flights are discussed in section 3.2.3 of this chapter, on AFSWC support missions at Shot FOX.

Project 6.4, Operational Tests of Radar and Photographic Techniques for IBDA, was conducted by the Wright Air Development

Page 53, 54, 55, 59, and 60 report DNA 6021F: the reason I'm putting these pages together is because we have discussed how the radiation dosage is measured and acquired in the Human body. First of all if you have a reading of 2.0 roentgens per hour (R/h) at ground zero, and you stand for 1 1/2 hours you will have 3.0 roentgens on your body, and your film badge will record 3.0 roentgens. So you see you will be OVERDOSED in 1 hour and 30 minutes for the whole year.

Let's look at it in a different prospective. In order to get to the 2.0 roentgens area, you are driven to the 1.0 roentgen area and then you hike at 1 1/2 miles per hour, with a full field pack to Ground Zero.

I will just quote a sentence from page 54 it says on this particular march to the display area. "At about 6:30 the troops were taken to the shot area." According to the map on page 53 the troops walked about 3 to 4 miles in and back out to the parking area.

In paragraph 2 on page 55 it does not give a definite time that they departed the shot area. It says "After viewing the equipment displays, the troops returned to the truck parking area for the trip to Camp Desert Rock." And try to understand the vagueness of this next statement. "The troops probably left the parking area at 9:30 A.M..

Like I say, if you look at pages 59 and 60 and read how high the radiation readings were, even the next day after the blast, it is unbelievable how much radiation a monitor received, just going in to get the readings and back out.

Even worse than the radiation he got on his film badge, think of the dust he swallowed, while driving around in circles for 3 hours (page 60) At readings up to 8.0 roentgens per hour. This was alpha and beta particles we were ingesting, and this radiation would not be recorded on the film badge.

Upon completion of their mission, the samplers returned to Indian Springs AFB and parked in the northeast corner of the parking area. Pilots then shut down the engines. The crews of the B-29s left the aircraft through the rear door between the stabilizer and the wing. The crews of the T-33s and F-84s disembarked by stepping onto a boarding ladder attached to the side of the aircraft. The sample-removing team and radiological safety monitors used long-handled tools to take samples from the aircraft and place them in shielded containers. They used the same method to remove the bottles containing the gaseous samples. They then loaded the sample containers onto courier aircraft for delivery to AEC laboratories for analysis (1-3; 36; 37; 52; 69).

Courier Missions

After the sampling missions had been completed, three B-25 and one C-47 aircraft left Indian Springs AFB and Yucca Lake airstrip on shot-day to transport samples and filter papers to various laboratories for analysis. The 4901st Support Wing (Atomic) conducted these courier missions.

At an unreported time, a B-25 flew from Indian Springs AFB to McClellan AFB with Project 7.3 samples. At 0800 hours, a C-47 flew from Indian Springs AFB to LASL with Program 13 samples. At about 0800 hours, a B-25 left Yucca Lake airstrip for LASL with Project 17.1 samples. At an unspecified time, a B-25 flew from Indian Springs AFB to the Army Chemical Center with Project 6.3 samples (1-3; 36; 37; 52; 69).

Cloud Tracking

Soon after the shot, one B-25 and one B-29 from Indian Springs AFB flew cloud-tracking missions over and beyond the NPG. The B-25 (tail number 099) took off at 0418 hours, tracked the cloud at altitudes ranging from 5,000 to 16,000 feet. and landed at 0805 hours. The B-29 (tail number 826) took off at 0415 hours, tracked the cloud at altitudes of 22,000 to 24,000 feet, and landed at 1018 hours (1-3; 36; 37; 52; 69).

3.3.1 Desert Rock Radiation Protection Activities

Personnel in the FOX observer program witnessed the detonation from trenches II kilometers from ground zero. The Desert Rock Radiological Safety Group devised plans and supplied personnel for radiation protection activities. Although the Army generally conducted these activities under the supervision of AFSWP monitors, Desert Rock monitors were permitted to survey the approach route to the display area without the supervision of AFSWP monitors. This was the first time in Operation TUMBLER-SNAPPER that Desert Rock monitors operated without AFSWP supervision (43; 51).

Orientation and Briefing

The indoctrination course, covering personal protection procedures and medical effects, as well as basic characteristics of nuclear weapons, was conducted from 12 to 24 May. The course was extended because adverse weather conditions and mechanical problems delayed the FOX detonation.-- For the first time in the series, members of the Instructor Group were from AFSWP. At the two previous shots with Desert Rock activities, instructors had not been familiar with the material that they presented (15; 51).

Dosimetry and Protective Equipment

The Signal Section issued film badges, which were supplied and processed by the AFSWP Radiological Safety Group, and the Quartermaster Section issued field protective masks to all participants. At the indoctrination course, <u>all personnel were instructed to place their film badges in their left breast pocket, with the numbers on the badge facing outward from the body· In addition, participants were instructed in the proper use of their field protective masks, which were to be wt,rn if the command was given to evacuate the area (49; 51)</u>

Monitoring

Following the detonation, Desert Rock monitors surveyed the approach route to the equipment display area. These monitors, unaccompanied by AFSWP monitors, noted radiation intensities along the route and located and marked the 0.5 R/h line, the forward limit for troops. After the monitors had surveyed the display route and AFSWP monitors had completed the survey of the rest of the shot area, the Test Manager declared the area safe to enter. Desert Rock monitors accompanied the troops as they moved up to and through the equipment display area (49; 51).

Decontamination

Personnel were brushed with brooms to remove contaminated dust when they returned from the trench area. Monitors then checked all personnel with AN/PDR-T1B meters. Those individuals whose readings could not be reduced to less than 0.01 R/h were ordered to the decontamination station at Yucca Pass to shower and change into clean clothing. Monitors checked these individuals after they had showered to ensure that intensities on their skin were less than 0.0015 R/h (49; 51).

Vehicles were also monitored and sent to the decontamination station if brushing could not reduce their level of contamination to less than 0.01 R/h (49; 51).

3.3.2 Joint AEC-DOD Radiation Protection Activities

Information on Shot FOX has been obtained from the radiological safety report prepared by AFSWP (43). The document includes data on radiological safety equipment. OhSite and offsite monitoring procedures, and radiation isointensity contour maps.

Page 76 report # DNA 6021F

In paragraph 2, and again remember shot Fox is the sixth shot, of the eight shot series, in this test. Paragraph Three just reinforces the credibility of how the tests were run, from two different reports.

"For the first time in the series, members of the instructor group were from AFSWP. At the two previous shots with Desert Rock activities, instructors had not been familiar with the material that they presented."

In paragraph 3 under "Dosimetry and Protective Equipment"

221

This again may not seem important, in itself, but it is another contradiction of-different-reports, on the identical activities. Here it says, "At the indoctrination course, all personnel were instructed to place their film badge in their left breast pocket, with the numbers on the badge facing outward from the body.

On page 156 of Report # DNA 6019F in paragraph # 3 it says. "The film badge, normally worn at chest level on the outside of the clothing, was designed to measure the wearers exposure to GAMMA radiation from external sources."

This statement is wrong, because, we did not have pins on the film badges to pin on our clothing. We had only the badge with a lead strip on the bottom of it. A bad problem with the earlier film badges that we were issued is, If the badge was accidentally turned around with the lead strip facing in, towards the body, YES, YOU GUESSED IT, no radiation reading on your film badge or on your recorded dosage.

Now on to the next page # 77 "Decontamination"

"Personnel were brushed with brooms to remove contaminated dust when they returned from the trench area." ..The worst thing that could happen to radiation is to stir it up, by brushing so that it is inhaled. If radiation is ingested or inhaled into your lungs, it may contaminate you for life. If you wear the contamination back to control point, and take a shower to get rid of it, at least then you are rid of it for life.

The letter I wrote home to my mother April 25,1952, that is a part of this book, explains that water cost the AEC $.07 per gallon to haul in from Las Vegas. that is as much as the price of gasoline was. In my letter home I stated that the AEC would not let us use water to wash the floors in our huts. Washing our "HUT" floors was considered excessive use of water. We were only allowed to sweep the floors of our living quarters.

Is it any wonder that the Army didn't want to use water on us, after all, IT WAS EXCESSIVE USE OF WATER. When brushing was cheaper. We were not worth our water. (or salt)..

Logistics and Materiel

During the period 25 through 31 May 1952, which covers the 25 May detonation of Shot FOX, the Logistics and Materiel Department issued film badges to about 340 AEC and DOD personnel involved in test group activities. The department also issued 549 sets of protective clothing and 260 radiation survey meters (43).

Monitoring

Initial ground survey monitors began recording radiation intensities at 0512 hours, slightly more than one hour after the detonation. They continued their survey until 0645 hours, approaching as close as 460 meters north of ground zero, where the radiation intensity was 10.0 R/h. Initial survey monitors, however, could not survey the area to the northeast of ground zero because of radiation levels in excess of 10.0 R/h. Monitors conducted resurveys on subsequent days. Part of the FOX radiation overlapped the residual radiation from Shot EASY, as indicated by the radiation contours to the south-southeast of ground zero (43).

Significant fallout also occurred northeast of the NPG, particularly in the area of Groom Mine, Nevada, about 30 kilometers from ground zero, where the highest recorded intensity was 0.32 R/h, seven hours after the detonation.

Eight to 13 two-man mobile teams participated in the offsite monitoring. About six hours before the detonation, they left the test area for assigned offsite locations.

In addition to the ground survey teams, two C-47s and two L-20s conducted offsite surveys of the terrain. The C-47 aircraft measured radiation intensities of up to 0.03 R/h approximately

<u>75 kilometers northeast of ground zero.</u> The highest radiation intensity encountered by the L-20s was 0.0025 R/h (43).

Page 78 Report # DNA 6021F

One of the reasons I would like you to look at this page is mainly to point out some of the hazards of working with the Atomic Bomb. The fact being that you can not smell, see. feel, or hear radiation contamination. So you do not know when your contamination is getting worse or better. You have only to rely on a man made machine to tell you when you are in trouble. The monitors were in the survey (the report says) from 5:12 A.M. until 6:45 A.M. at Ground Zero.

Now if each monitor went in as far as he was supposed to, and that is 10.0 R/h, and mind you they had to take readings and record them every 100 yards, for later mapping of Ground Zero. It is impossible for me to believe after spending all of the time I did in the desert how anyone can do this job without getting overdosed, on just one shot. A person is only supposed to receive 3.0 R/h for the whole year. If you spent **just 10 minutes going in, 10 minutes taking readings, and 10 minutes coming out,** <u>and mind you all of this time is driving on the desert which is slow driving. You would have a minimum of 5.0 R/h,</u> which is almost twice the limit. Who is kidding whom, it doesn't make it mathematically in my books, **This is impossible for me to believe, even on an interstate highway.**

While we are in this paragraph it says "part of the FOX radiation overlapped the <u>residual radiation from shot EASY"</u> this is proof that what I said earlier in this book. We drove across the desert <u>every day</u> across the former Ground Zeros And did not even have film badges.

If the two contaminated areas overlapped and shot EASY was still contaminated after shot FOX was detonated, the two shots were detonated almost 3 weeks apart. (EASY was detonated May 7, 1952 FOX was detonated May 25, 1952

I am really saddened that the 369th engineers were out there installing heavy equipment and tests, without film badges before shot FOX while the radiation was present, and the AEC had to know it. I can't believe the AEC wouldn't know they were going to overlap another radiation area. Why were we out there every day mapping radiation areas. I sometimes wonder if their job was just to blow up bombs, and let the chips fall where they may. **What kind of results can the AEC expect with one bomb on top of another one ??**

Page 136 report DNA 6019F, that we have covered, states, "film badges were only issued to official reentry parties, and other personnel entering a CONTROLLED radiation area."

These poor fellows had the same amount of protection the 216th had. **That was none.** We just didn't fit in with the good guys. (the ones that were not issued Film Badges, but were **AWARDED** a film badge.) cartridge belts with a canteen. They carried field protective masks and individual weapons (17; 53; 78).

From 60 minutes before the detonation to about 15 minutes after shot-time, a Desert Rock instructor gave information and final instructions to the troops over the public address system Two minutes before shot-time, he ordered all personnel to crouch in their trenches, cover theft faces with their hands, lean against the forward trench wall, and remain below ground level until after the detonation (17; 51; 78).

Three seconds after the flash of light from the detonation a: 0355 hours, the instructor cleared all personnel to stand up and view the fireball and cloud. Approximately 20 seconds, after the shot, the blast wave reached the trench area and the resulting dust obscured vision temporarily (17; 51; 78). '

In addition to the troops in the trenches, there were five tanks with crews from the 1st Armored Division in the shot area. These tanks had moved to a position Just east of the trench area during the 12 hours before the detonation. The crews remained in their tanks during the detonation. Immediately after the blast wave passed, the tanks started their engines and, on orders from

225

the Exercise Director, moved forward to attack the objective south of ground zero. Figure 4-1 shows the probable route of this maneuver (51).

Also by order of the Exercise Director and without requiring an AEC radiological safety clearance, the maneuver troops left the trenches. The troops were divided into two groups. They advanced on foot in column formation along the two roads leading to the GEORGE shot area, as shown in figure 4-1. The tanks and one 1/4-ton communications vehicle led each column. Desert Rock CBR monitors accompanied each group to the shot area 51/ 74).

Page 90 of report # DNA 6021F :

This page is very important. There is one sentence on 89 that is a part of the first paragraph on page # 90.

Page # 89 "Tactical troops wore fatigues, combat boots, steel helmets, field Jackets, and" (page # 90) "cartridge belts with a canteen. They carried field protective masks and individual weapons."

These troops had none of the protective clothing, that is talked about all during these reports. In all reality, what is the difference in fatigues or a pair of coveralls? Except the coveralls are called "protective clothing." I have never heard nor seen a "field protective mask", also I didn't have a gas mask, and I didn't see any one else in the field with one during the whole series of Tumbler-Snapper.

Three seconds after the detonation the troops were ordered to stand up in their trenches. If the shock wave hit 17 seconds after the troops stood up, I Would have thought the exercise director put these men in harms way, because of flying debris.

Immediately after the shock wave passed, "by order of the exercise director and WITHOUT REQUIRING AN AEC RADIOLOGICAL SAFETY CLEARANCE, THE MANEUVER TROOPS LEFT THE TRENCHES." They advanced on foot to the George Shot Area."

Again in my opinion the "Exercise Director" is showing complete disregard of the troops health, both, mentally and

226

physically, just a few minutes, after he ordered them to stand up against the shock wave. He ordered them to move into Ground Zero, "without requiring an AEC Radiological Safety Clearance."

I will Quote one sentence from page # 91 about this same maneuver after the "troops and tanks returned to the parking area where they were **PROBABLY MONITORED FOR RADIATION before returning to Desert Rock.**"

Page # 88 says that the 369th was attached to the 1st Armored Division and was a part of this exercise

This "Exercise Director" of this exercise evidently, were using these troops in a combat situation when it was not called for. In other words, the troops were used as "Guinea Pigs." He had absolutely no concern or remorse for his actions...

This gives me a sick feeling, and someone else was sick to order these troops to do this type of exercise. On the other hand it may have been the **"Test Director himself"** and the exercise director had to follow orders, even if it meant his own health or life.

THE TEST DIRECTOR DID KNOW BETTER, BUT CHOSE TO CLOSE HIS EYES.

If the records were so poorly kept that the AEC could not keep track of a B-29 Bomber airplane, by not even recording the tail number on flights over Ground Zero, immediately after the detonation, How could they keep track of a film badge, name, or serial number of a servicemen ??

Cloud Tracking

Soon after the detonation, one B-25 and two 8-29s from Indian Springs AFB flew cloud-tracking missions over and beyond the Nevada Proving Ground. The B-25 (tail number 099) took off at 0418 hours, tracked the cloud at heights ranging from 900 to 14,000 feet, and landed at 0905 hours. The B-29 (tail

227

number unknown) took off at 0410 hours and landed at 1155 hours. The second B-29 (tail number 826) left at 0917 hours tracked the cloud at heights ranging from 18,000 to 22,000 feet, and landed at 1300 hours. The C-47 (tail number unknown) left at 0650 hours add returned at 1255 hours. The flight profile of the C-47 is not known (1-3; 38; 37; 52; 69).

Aerial Surveys of Terrain

After the detonation, two C-47s and one L-20 aircraft, all based at Indian Springs AFB, conducted radiological surveys of the onsite and offsite terrain. One C-47 (tail number 386) left at 0630 hours, flew at 300 to 1,500 feet above the terrain, and returned at 1125 hours. A second C-47 aircraft (tail number 308) took off at 0650 hours, flew at heights of 1,000 to 10,000 feet, and landed at 1255 hours. The L-20 (tail number 467) took off at 0530 hours, conducted its survey at 100 to 500 feet above the terrain, and landed at 0805 hours (1-3; 36; 37; 52; 69).

Observer Activities

Observers from the Strategic Air Command participated in an orientation and indoctrination exercise in nuclear weapons effects. On shot-day, two B-5Os, possibly from Carswell AFB, Texas, with SAC observers onboard entered the Nevada Proving Ground area between PlO0 and 0300 hours. One B-50 aircraft remained in an orbiting pattern through shot-time to allow the observers to witness the detonation and subsequent cloud development. This aircraft left the shot area at 0400 hours to return to its base. The other B-50 conducted a weather 0925 hours to perform a special radiological safety mission. It returned to Indian Springs at 1155 hours, and then proceeded to the Yucca Lake airstrip. The aircraft then returned to Indian Springs, arriving at 1238 hours (1-3; 36; 37; 54; 69). **The activities of the second L-20 are not known.** *(The AEC didn't keep very good track of us servicemen.)*

Observers

The crew of one SAC aircraft, a B-36 possibly from Carswell AFB, Texas, witnessed the HOW detonation. The 8-36 entered the area over the NPG at 0338 hours and left the area at 0408 hours (I-3; 5; 36; 37; *52;* 69).

5.2 RADIATION PROTECTION AT SHOT HOW

The primary purpose of the radiation protection procedures developed by the test groups and AFSWC for Operation TUMBLER-SNAPPER was to keep individual exposures to ionizing radiation to a minimum, while still allowing participants to accomplish their missions.

Logistics and Materiel

From 5 June to 9 June 1952, which covers the 5 June detonation of Shot HOW, the Logistics and Materiel Department issued 300 sets of protective clothing and 250 radiation survey meters. The department also issued film badges (43).

Monitoring

The initial ground survey team began recording radiation intensities at 0545 hours. The survey was completed along all but the north stake line by 0700 hours. Measurements were made along the north stake line between 0915 and 0940 hours. Winds resulted in a large amount of fallout northwest of the shot area, but no effort was made to complete the survey in that direction since early recovery operations were not necessary there (43).

(Paul Martin was sent here in Error and overdosed.)
After reading the previous page 167, please turn back to Paul A. Martin's letter, that he wrote to me on

229

pages 54 and 55 of this book. Keep in mind, these 40 men were writing to me from all parts of the country, with absolutely no knowledge of what their buddies were writing, or later on what I would find in the Government Records. You'll see how good the equipment was that we had to work with. The truck that was assigned to Paul and his partner broke down and their radio quit working at Ground Zero. No one knew they were even out there in this extremely high radiation area, but they were sent out there by the AEO to measure the radiation levels on the <u>NORTH & NORTHWEST LINES.</u>

I have kept telling how poorly this whole project was run, and right here is another prime example, of either stupidity, unconcern for troops lives, or like so many times no one checking or supervising. With lives in the hands of the director, you would have thought he would have had more competent men under him..It could be possible (again) that he really considered these problems to bothersome to waste his time checking on.

Page 144 Quote, "Measurements were made along the north stake line between 0915 and 0940 hours. (25 minutes) Winds resulted in a large amount of fallout Northwest of the shot area, but no effort was made to complete the survey in that direction since early recovery operations were not necessary there." BUT Paul was sent in there to monitor the Northwest line. On page 144 is a radiation map of Shot How. I would imagine when the control point couldn't reach anyone on the northwest line the test director had to come up with a good excuse, why they didn't have any readings on the Northwest line. The best excuse was, well, We really didn't need the readings, because we had no instruments there. Then I have to say, why did the AEC send Paul in ? ? I will put page 144 at the bottom of this page.

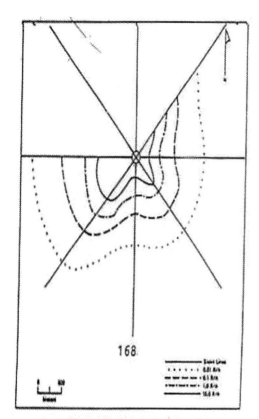

168.

Figure 5-4: INITIAL RADIATION ISOINTENSITY MAP FOR SHOT HOW
8 JUNE 1952, 0600 HOURS

231

About the Author

I have worked over 4, 000 hours in the past 5 years, since the sealed records were opened, trying to get the Government to recognize the physical problems of the "Atomic Veterans." I testified twice in front of the U.S Senate. Once on Aug. 5,1994 and once on April 21,1998 on illnesses caused by radiation, to our American Veterans. I served my country during the Korean War in 1950-'51-'52. I was the Mayor for two terms (6 years) 1988-1994. I was member (up to President) for 10 years of the Lions International. I have been a member of the American Legion for 40 + years. I am church member, a Deacon, and also serve in the Prison Ministry. MY BOOK "RADIATION THE SILENT KILLER" WAS ACCEPTED INTO THE ETERNAL RECORDS OF THE U.S SENATE ON APR. 21,1998. ALSO IN THE LIBRARY OF CONGRESS #Txu 837-607.

LaVergne, TN USA
09 November 2009
163570LV00001B/1/A